THE EUROPEAN HISTORY SERIES

SERIES EDITOR

KEITH EUBANK

D1611619

ARTHUR S. LINK
GENERAL EDITOR FOR HISTORY

CHURCH AND STATE

IN TUDOR AND STUART ENGLAND

STUART E. PRALL

QUEENS COLLEGE

AND THE GRADUATE SCHOOL

AND UNIVERSITY CENTER

CITY UNIVERSITY OF NEW YORK

HARLAN DAVIDSON, INC.

ARLINGTON HEIGHTS, ILLINOIS 60004

BR
756
.P735
1993

Library of Congress Cataloging-in-Publication Data

Prall, Stuart E.
    Church and state in Tudor and Stuart England / Stuart E. Prall.
        p. cm. — (The European history series)
    Includes bibliographical references and index.
    ISBN 0-88295-904-2
    1. Church and state—England—History—16th century.   2. Church and
state—England—History—17th century.   3. England—Church history—16th
century.   4. England—Church history—17th century.   5. Great
Britain—History—Tudors, 1485–1603.   6. Great Britain—History—Stuarts,
1603–1714.   I. Title.   II. Series: European history series (Arlington Heights,
Ill.)
BR756.P735 1993
274.2'06—dc20   92-35135
                                                                                       CIP

Cover illustration: After Hogarth, Henry VIII and Anne Boleyn. *Bridgeman/
Art Resource, N.Y.*

Manufactured in the United States of America
97 96 95 94 93 1 2 3 4 5 MG

FOREWORD

Now more than ever there is a need for books dealing with significant themes in European history, books offering fresh interpretations of events which continue to affect Europe and the world. The end of the Cold War has changed Europe, and to understand the changes, a knowledge of European history is vital. Although there is no shortage of newspaper stories and television reports about politics and life in Europe today, there is a need for interpretation of these developments as well as background information that neither television nor newspapers can provide. At the same time, scholarly interpretations of European history itself are changing.

A guide to understanding Europe begins with knowledge of its history. To understand European history is also to better understand much of the American past because many of America's deepest roots are in Europe. And in these days of increasingly global economic activity, more American men and women journey to Europe for business as well as personal travel. In both respects, knowledge of European history can deepen one's understanding, experience, and effectiveness.

The European History Series introduces readers to the excitement of European history through concise books about the great events, issues, and personalities of Europe's past. Here are accounts of the powerful political and religious movements which shaped European life in the past and which have influenced events in Europe today. Colorful stories of rogues and heroines, tyrants, rebels, fanatics, generals, statesmen, kings, queens, emperors, and ordinary people are contained in these concise studies of major themes and problems in European history.

Each volume in the series examines an issue, event, or era which posed a problem of interpretation for historians. The chosen topics are neither obscure nor narrow. These books are neither historiographical essays, nor substitutes for textbooks, nor monographs with endless numbers of footnotes. Much thought and care have been given to their writing style to avoid academic jargon and overspecialized focus. Authors of the European History Series have been selected not only for their recognized scholarship but also for their ability to write for the general reader. Using primary and secondary sources in their writing, these authors bring alive the great moments in European history rather than simply cram factual material into the pages of their books. The authors combine more in-depth interpretation than is found in the usual survey accounts with synthesis of the finest scholarly works, but, above all, they seek to write absorbing historical narrative.

Each volume contains a bibliographical essay which introduces readers to the most significant works dealing with their subject. These are works that are generally available in American public and college libraries. It is hoped that the bibliographical essays will enable readers to follow their interests in further reading about particular pieces of the fascinating European past described in this series.

Keith Eubank
Series Editor

CONTENTS

v i i

CONTENTS / ix

PREFACE

For many generations historians have sought to find the point or points at which the transition from medieval to modern times took place. At one time the Protestant Reformation was seen as the culmination of the Renaissance and the beginning of the modern era. At another time, the emergence of the centralized and bureaucratized nation-state was the crucial factor. More recently, historians have tended to view scientific developments as being the most important determinants of the distinction between medieval and modern. However one views the problem, most historians would agree that 1500 found Europe essentially medieval and 1700 found it essentially modern.

Wherever the historian seeks the answer to the transition question, two institutions and the ideas surrounding them come into focus: "church" and "state." The terms "church" and "state" in the title of this book refer to what medieval scholars saw as the "two swords" by which God's rule over this world was effected: the spiritual sword (the church) and the secular sword (the state). The relationship between the two and the powers assigned to each in relation to the other had been the stuff of perpetual debate and countless wars throughout the Middle Ages. In medieval Europe, the church generally occupied the central position and the state played a subordinate role. During the sixteenth and seventeenth centuries, the church went through a crisis that resulted in the split between Roman Catholics and Protestants. These same centuries also saw the Scientific Revolution, which had the effect of so changing views about God, and therefore about the church, that the state finally was able to take the offensive and become the new locus of authority.

This book tells the story of how the transition from the centrality of the church to that of the state occurred in Tudor and Stuart England. The story begins with a quite medieval Henry VIII and ends with the triumph of constitutional/parliamentary monarchy following the Glorious Revolution of 1688–1689. Besides a Bill of Rights, the first step taken by the new regime led by William and Mary was the passage of the Toleration Act of 1689 (for Protestants). From then on the state was the unifying factor and the church became a divisive factor.

This book will examine the church-state relationship on three levels: the institutional level, where both the church and the state are considered; the constitutional (legal) level, where the rights and obligations of each toward the believer/citizen are examined; and the psychosocial level, where beliefs and practices are discussed in terms of human conduct and needs. The story is a complex one. The levels are interrelated, and it is not possible to understand any one level without considering its relationships with the other two.

Stuart Prall

INTRODUCTION: MEDIEVAL AND MODERN VIEWS OF GOD

The greatest obstacle to our understanding of life in the centuries preceding our own is the failure to understand how our predecessors viewed God and what religion meant to them. Even those of us who are religious in some traditional sense do not really comprehend what God and religious beliefs meant in the prescientific era. Historians are increasingly convinced that the Tudor-Stuart centuries were essentially medieval. Although the Protestant Reformation was long viewed as the sharp divide between the medieval and the modern, the more recent view sees the Scientific Revolution as being the dividing point. Whether one was Catholic or Protestant was of less importance in the long run than whether or not one believed in an immanent God. Luther and Calvin were God-centered men who assumed that God was an active, indeed the dominant, force in the life of the universe, each and every moment of our existence. The centuries after Newton were not so God-centered. The centuries outlined in this book can only be understood if we first see how those who lived in that world saw God and the role God played in their world.

The medieval church had totally incorporated within itself the scientific teachings of the ancient Greeks and Romans. Aristotle's portrayal of the Prime Mover (the unmoved mover) is philosophically identical to the Judeo-Christian portrayal of God (the uncreated creator). Aristotle's definition of inertia was a crucial element in the structure. Where we have accepted the Newtonian definition that the status quo is the norm (an object at rest remains at rest; an object in motion remains in motion) requiring intervention only to effect change, the Aristotelian system called for rest to be the norm, and therefore all motion required intervention. A universe in perpetual motion required a perpetual application of energy. Aristotelian physics therefore totally complemented the Church's assertion that God was creator, mover, protector, defender, author, and determiner of all things from one moment to the next. All life on this planet and the movement of the stars and other planets depended at every instance upon the work of God.

The ancient Ptolemaic design of the universe was geocentric or earth centered. A system of science which considered earth, air, fire, and water to be the four fundamental elements naturally led to the assumption that "earth" was not only the ingredient for our own planet but was the center of the whole universe. If "earth" was the heaviest of all elements (gravity), then the heavenly bodies in motion, being without gravity, but having levity, would revolve around that object which was heavy. Aristotle's and Ptolemy's universes were one and had been totally adopted by the medieval Church. Earth was at the center of a universe originally created by God and continually "moved" by God. The Bible had added the belief that this world was the special domain of humankind, who had been created by God and given dominion over the birds of the air, the fish of the sea, and all that was in between. Man was the ruler of the earth. Given the natural hierarchy among men, some were higher than others. The highest ranking human, the pope, could claim to be next to God in the universal order of things. The only challenge to this came from the occasional emperor or king who would substitute himself for the pope.

God's role was so completely understandable in terms of medieval science that only a person ignorant of that science could question God's centrality and God's immanence. The Scientific Revolution that culminated with Sir Isaac Newton and the modern definition of inertia moved God further and further away from being the perpetual mover. He ended up being the creator and, perhaps, a judge at the end, with little, if any, role in between. No one today really believes the sun rose this morning only because of a deliberate act by God. Tudor-Stuart Englishmen did! That is the difference between then and now!

Many scholars now see the decline, and perhaps the eclipse, of religion and the controlling authority of an immanent God being replaced by a new center of authority. The God (and the Church) of a geocentric medieval world has been replaced by a world where authority is centralized in an increasingly bureaucratic centralized nation-state, under the suzerainty of a monarch in the years prior to the French Revolution. A sure sign of this change is that the supreme crime, punishable by death, is no longer heresy. In modern times it is treason! Tudor-Stuart England is a microcosm of this transition.

The Henrician Reformation and the replacement of the Church in England by the Church of England* under the supremacy of a "divine-right" monarch provided a stage upon which all these new forces at work in Europe could be and were played out. The English Reformation was different from those on the Continent, but England witnessed everything the others did. Only in England was the whole story played out in all its splendor!

---

* "Church in England" refers to the English branch of the Universal Roman Catholic Church; "Church of England" is the name acquired after the separation from the Roman Church.

1 / PRE-REFORMATION CHURCH AND STATE

Henry VIII came to the throne in 1509 as a youth of eighteen who had already earned a reputation as both a Prince Charming and a "Renaissance man." As the second son of Henry VII, he had not been born to be king, and his education had been geared toward the possibility that he might become a bishop of the church. All formal education in the Middle Ages revolved around religion and the church. Henry, however, had received more than the usual religious training, although there is no solid evidence as to how he actually acquired his fluency in matters religious.

The English nation was typically medieval in the way in which religion and the wider culture were completely entwined. The lives of the people and the structure of its institutions were so mingled that any thought of separating one from the other was preposterous. In terms of the nation's links with the wider Catholic world, the English were fully aligned with the universal church centered at Rome. Ever since the Great Schism (1378–1413) that had followed the long period of the Avignon papacy, the English had become firmly allied to the Roman papacy. The years of a French papacy had led to strains, and when England had had to choose between a pope in Rome and a pope in Avignon, the choice was not only clear, but the ties to Rome were woven ever more tightly. England was considered to be the most loyal supporter of the Roman papacy in Western Europe. This alliance was to remain strong until the middle of the reign of Henry VIII. The break between the English and the Roman church was not expected. How far it might have been anticipated is one of the great historical questions.

Before proceeding further, it is necessary to outline briefly but fully the basic teachings of the Christian church as they were understood by the late medieval world. The basic points of theology so completely underlay the culture and its institutions that any understanding of the Tudor-Stuart world requires a firm grasp of those basic teachings. As was said above, people in this era really believed in God. They also really believed in Christianity as the true religion. There might be differences about many parts of the whole and complex package, but there was total agreement about certain fundamentals. The basic Christian message had been outlined in the early fifth century by St. Augustine in his short handbook, *The Enchiridion.* He wrote that human beings were the descendants of Adam and Eve after their expulsion from the Garden of Eden, or Paradise. To be human was to be a punishment for sin. Where Adam and Eve had been "created" in the image of God, their descendants are born as humans and will die as humans. Death will be followed by an eternity in Hell. A just God gives humans what they deserve— everlasting damnation. But God is merciful as well as just and provides a means of overcoming Hell and assuring salvation, or the reunion with God in Heaven. The goal of all humans is to overcome Original Sin and the expulsion from Paradise and to be restored to Paradise. How this salvation was to be accomplished was the crucial issue in theology.

The Catholic church taught that salvation was achieved by a combination of faith and good works. Faith meant the acceptance of Jesus as the Christ or messiah. More particularly, it meant the acceptance of Jesus as the one true God who temporarily took on human nature, was born of a woman (without a human father), lived, died (violently, by crucifixion), and on the third day after death rose from the dead, assuming a state analogous to that of Adam and Eve before the Fall. The risen Christ then ascended to Heaven and was reunited with the Father and the Holy Spirit, being recognized as the Son, the second person of the Trinity. Belief in Jesus the Christ, born, died, and resurrected, was necessary for salvation, yet such belief was beyond the competence of a normal human being. Christ was so far beyond humankind that he was beyond human comprehension. The true faith could be attained only by an act of God. The faith was God's gift, given through grace. Salvation was, therefore, a gift of God. The grace of God was transmitted through the sacraments of the church (the good works), which were divinely ordained, miraculous ceremonies performed by clergy whose ordinations were themselves miraculous sacraments passing on the authority originally given by Jesus to the twelve apostles. The church and its clergy were therefore the divine agents by whose sacramental ministrations the faith could be transmitted and strengthened among the ordinary sinners on earth. The human goal was to be reunited with God in Heaven. The divinely appointed agents assisting in the accomplishment of that goal were the church, its clergy, and its sacraments.

The Reformation came about because of a bitter split among churchmen as to whether or not the true faith, being the gift of God, is something that a person receives only passively or by a conscious act on his own part. The legacy of St. Augustine could lead to the Catholic teaching that the human sinner can choose to participate in the sacraments or not. By making such a choice, a person was choosing to actively participate in his own salvation. Those who were to become Protestants claimed that God alone was the sole determiner of salvation and had in fact made the decision in each individual case at the very beginning of creation. The Catholic church insisted that humans had some role to play in salvation; at least they could choose to be good Catholics. For the Protestant, God alone was the author of one's fate. The Catholic tradition came to be called free will; the Protestant came to be known as predestination. The Protestant theologians saw this matter as a zero-sum game: any role for the human in determining the ultimate fate was seen as reducing the role of God. From the Protestant point of view, the Catholics were diminishing the sovereignty of God. From the Catholic point of view, predestination made the sacraments and the clergy instituted by God superfluous. The Catholic link between free will and the sacraments was fundamental, and the belief in free will thus meant the acceptance of the clergy as God's instruments of salvation. This led to a church and culture of overweening clerics who dispensed sacraments to a passive laity in return for great sums of money. Free will could be seen as the bright side of a corrupt and corrupting priest-ridden church in that it did allow the individual to have some role to play in achieving salvation; the ability to choose or not to choose to follow the practices of the church. The Reformation was not just a dispute among theologians; it was a struggle over the souls of human beings.

The medieval church was a highly complex structure with a clear-cut division between the clergy who administered the sacraments and the laity who received them. The clergy was organized in a hierarchical structure, with power and authority flowing from the top (pope and/or king) down. The Catholic church traced its descent from the appearance of the Holy Ghost to the apostles at Pentecost, ten days after the ascension of Jesus. The apostles were regarded as being the first bishops, who had the duty and the ability to teach and preach the truth of the gospel and to administer the miraculous sacraments. The bishop administered a diocese, within which were parish churches administered by priests. The archbishops were either bishops with jurisdiction over other bishops or were bishops of particularly prestigious dioceses. The priest came from the people of the community and ministered to the community. He was generally from the rural working class or peasantry and was appointed to his "living" by the landlord or some successor to the original landlord who had purchased or been awarded the appointing power (the advowson). The priest baptized, heard confessions, said Mass, performed marriages, and administered the Last Rites and the burying of the dead. All but the burial were sacraments by which the priest assisted God in transmitting the saving grace to the laity.

The priest was subordinate to the bishop, even if not chosen by the bishop. The bishop alone could perform the sacraments of Confirmation and Holy Orders (the service in which one entered into the office of deacon, priest, or bishop). The bishop also enforced the collection of the tithe, which was supposed to be equally divided among the parish, the bishop, and the charitable offerings of the church. In addition, the bishop presided over the diocesan or bishop's court, which handled all cases involving clergy and cases involving the laity where a religious issue was in dispute. Because matrimony was a sacrament, all court cases concerning eligibility for marriage and annulment of a marriage were dealt with in the ecclesiastical court. Likewise, because the Last Rites was a sacrament, the probating of wills was reserved for the bishop's court. The most contentious issue was the scope of benefit of clergy. Since punishments in church courts were generally more lenient than those in the secular courts, it was to the advantage of an accused person to be recognized as having clerical status and, thus, be tried in the church court. Literacy had become accepted as one such proof of clerical status. The king, and the laity in general, were never happy to see known criminals get off leniently in church courts because of their ability to qualify for "benefit of clergy." From the twelfth to the sixteenth centuries, the crown gradually reduced the number of crimes for which this immunity could be claimed. Murder still remained such a crime in the sixteenth century. As the crimes for which benefit of clergy could be claimed were reduced, the church expanded the number of laity who could qualify as clergy by making the literacy test increasingly simple. The test for literacy had become standardized and required no more than the recitation from memory of Psalm 82:2: "How long will ye give wrong judgment, and accept the persons of the ungodly?" The claim of benefit of clergy could only be used once in a murder case, and the result was that a man could commit "one free murder." This, naturally, annoyed the king and the citizenry interested in law and order.

The kingdom of England at the accession of Henry VIII was composed of two ancient archbishoprics—Canterbury and York—and fifteen bishoprics. All the archbishops and bishops had seats in the House of Lords, as did the abbots of the "greater" monasteries. The archbishops and bishops were elected by the cathedral chapters (or the clergy assigned to the cathedral) after being nominated by the king. Before assuming office, however, the bishop or archbishop had to be approved by the pope, who alone could remove him from office. Besides a seat in the House of Lords, the archbishops and bishops often served as general advisers with membership of the Council (known as the Privy Council since the reign of Henry VIII). One or more of the ranking prelates also served in a particular office of state, such as lord chancellor. Cardinal Wolsey was to be the last, but one, of these clerical lord chancellors, but other offices were still occasionally bestowed on the clergy through the reign of Elizabeth I.

The church in England was a central part of the life of the local community and of the nations on the highest level, and was
also part of the Western European Roman church. In addition to
having the final say over the appointment and removal of all
bishops and archbishops, the pope also had a role in selecting
some monastic abbots and even some parish priests. The pope
also was the capstone of the ecclesiastical court system; all
cases could be appealed from the court of the archbishop to that
of the Holy Father in Rome. In some cases, such as annulments,
Rome had primary jurisdiction. The pope, of course, was the
"keeper of the keys," the guardian of the faith, and the supreme
teacher. Bulls and encyclicals might be issued from Rome at any
time and on almost any subject.

The attempts, at the time of the Great Schism, to restrict the
pope's powers and restrain him by the use of church councils
had failed. The years from 1305–1378 have forever after been
known as the period of "Babylonian Captivity" of the papacy,
when it was centered in Avignon, France, rather than in Rome.
The decision to return to Rome in 1378 resulted in the election of
a pope in Rome and one in Avignon. This split, or Great Schism,
lasted for many years (including several popes in each city), cul-
minating in the restoration of a simple Roman papacy in 1414.
This restoration was accomplished by the decision reached at
the Council of Constance, at which time the Council also decreed that all popes should govern with the advice and consent
of church councils. By the middle of the fifteenth century the
popes had succeeded in resuming absolute power and putting an
end to the "Conciliar Movement." The English kings had always supported the Roman rather than the Avignon or French
popes during the Great Schism and also supported the pope in
opposition to the councils. There was thus one true pope in
Rome exercising a *plenitudo potestatis* (full authority), and the
English kings were true to him, in their fashion. The fashion was
that the crown supported the church in the collection of the tithe
and in the collection and payment to Rome of the *annates* (first
fruits), which was a year's revenue from a diocese that was pay-
able to the pope when a new bishop took office. The sum was, of
course, indirectly a tax upon the residents of the diocese.

The close ties between Rome and the English kings had been a reaction to the French popes during the Hundred Years' War, when the papacy was in Avignon. During these years, Parliament had enacted laws that put limits on those ties. The Acts of Provisors of 1351 and 1390 forbade direct papal appointment to any posts within the English church, except when the crown itself might share in the profits. The Acts of *Praemunire* of 1353, 1365, and 1393 barred legal appeals to Rome if they were in any way considered to be against the interest of the crown. The English kings preferred a Roman pope to a French one, and they preferred a pope free from the restraints of a council, just as the kings themselves preferred to be free from the restraints of either councils or parliaments. The flow of English cash to Rome was acceptable as long as the king got financial and/or political benefits in return. The newly installed Lancastrian king, Henry IV, sought support for his throne by backing the passage of the Statute *De Heretico Comburendo* (or the Burning of Heretics) in 1401. Thus England joined the Continent in the burning of heretics, although in England heresy was a crime against the state as well as the church, making a separate inquisition unnecessary.

The institutional establishment culminated in the practical alliance at the top of king and pope, with the king uppermost in authority. On the lowest level of the hierarchy, the parish was developing into a unit of local government. Prior to the break from Rome, the parish had been largely a religious entity led by the priest. The dissolution of the monasteries, as we shall see later, resulted in the state moving into the charitable vacuum created by the dissolutions. The state, in turn, assigned the parish and its lay leaders more and more duties for the relief of the poor. For example, the Poor Tax was to be collected and distributed on the parish level. This additional responsibility was really a logical extension of the work done by the late medieval church wardens, who saw to the functioning of nearly all aspects of the parish life other than the liturgical.

Religion in late medieval England was a highly complex combination of elements—dogmas, rituals, persons, structures, and monies—that claimed to be God's instrument for leading individual sinners to salvation in the next world. These elements were part and parcel of the life of each individual and of every level of organized public life, from the local village or manor up to the king and his court. No one, from top to bottom, was to doubt that all of this was, or at least ought to be, serving the joint needs of God and man. Since the fourteenth century, however, there were increasingly vocal and occasionally even violent criticisms of or attacks upon the dogmas, rituals, persons, structures, or monies, or any combination of them, sparked by disgust with corruption or because of secular rulers' dislike of clerical pretentions to power. One of the great and continuing controversies among historians is the extent to which pre-Reformation England was ripe for a Reformation. The traditional view is that the Reformation was both an affair of state and was imposed upon the nation by the king. Alternative theories have stressed just the opposite: that England was already prepared for a Reformation by the people themselves. It is not a simple matter to take one position or the other on this issue. To a great extent the problem results from a difference of opinion as to just what the Reformation was all about. How one views pre-Reformation England is greatly influenced by how one views the Reformation itself. It will be useful at this point to survey the problem in greater depth.

THE SEEDS OF CONFLICT

Throughout its long history, the Catholic church has oscillated between two views of how to motivate the laity toward a greater acceptance of the teachings and the practices of the church. The views might be considered analogous to the "carrot" versus the "stick"; they also might be considered analogous to the symbol of the cross itself.

The carrot-and-stick analogy is centered on the relative importance of Hell. Should the church encourage a good Christian life by stressing the joys of salvation with Christ in Heaven (the carrot) or the horrors of an eternity in Hell with the Devil (the stick)? Over the centuries the emphasis has moved back and forth like a pendulum. The emphasis on the joys of salvation led the laity to trust in God's saving mercy, thus resulting in a more lax conformity. The fear of Hell, on the other hand, led to a mechanical reliance on the quantity, but not the quality, of sacramental participation, as well as the sale of indulgences (the remission of time in purgatory) and the "purchase" of salvation. The fear of Hell also led to a general despondency and even resignation, which were not healthy.

The analogy to the cross is different, but also could have mixed results. The horizontal and vertical bars of the cross could be seen as pointers, with the vertical leading one's eyes and thoughts upward to God and Heaven and the horizontal directing one's eyes and thoughts to the neighbors on either side. The church could teach the need to look in both directions simultaneously, but that had proven to be impossible for most people. Each person tends to stress one line of vision over the other, and the church over the centuries has put its own stress upon one direction or the other. Does each person look primarily to God and his own salvation, or does he see himself as part of a community that worships and lives together? The vertical approach stressed the lone sinner turning to God through the medium of the clergy performing sacraments. The horizontal approach stressed the community and was consistent with the claim that the church was the body of the faithful, not just a body of ordained clergy. The late medieval church was increasingly torn between the two approaches; they were, in fact, becoming two separate camps.

The church as a hierarchically arranged body of clergy performing sacraments had achieved dominance in the reign of pope Innocent III (1198–1216). Church architecture had developed in response to this hierarchical structure: the High Gothic cathedral directed one's focus Heavenward. The Gothic cathedrals and the new parish churches screened off the sanctuary where the priest said Mass, so that the lay congregation could barely, if at all, see the priest at the altar. If the laity could hear the priest, it heard him speaking in a foreign language (Latin); how much was understood is open to question. During the Mass, an ordained and celibate priest performed the miracle of transubstantiation; he converted bread and wine into the body and blood of Christ. Jesus was, in fact, dying over and over again, each time Mass was said. What for the church was the central event in human history, the death of Christ, was repeated for the benefit of mankind in an unknown tongue behind an almost impenetrable screen that blocked all views and most sound. The laity rarely received the bread (body); the wine (blood) was reserved for the clergy.

The separation of laity and clergy in the Mass was a culmination of a historical process that originated in the institution of infant baptism. By making church membership contingent upon nothing more than birth, the whole idea of involvement and personal commitment was missing. And the recipient of the Last Rites was often unconscious, or barely conscious. Thus, birth and death were treated mechanically by the church; the Mass joined them as yet another automatic ritual. Thus, in practicing religion, the laity attended certain rituals on certain occasions; feasted and fasted according to the church's calendar; was married and buried according to the rules of the church; prayed to or honored saints according to the dates and prayers assigned; confessed according to prescribed formulae; and attended, but did not participate in, the Mass. Critics of this system became very numerous in the fourteenth century. John Wycliffe, a priest and philosopher, expressed several bases upon which opposition could be built. One was to challenge the sacramental system; another, growing out of this, was to challenge the church's claims to supremacy in relation to the state. One result of this growing opposition was the emergence of groups that put new emphasis upon the laity, claiming that the body of believers constituted the real "body of Christ."

Wycliffe denied the supremacy of the church over the state (supporting Edward III in his opposition to the papacy in Avignon) by denying the sacramental nature of clerical ordination. If Holy Orders were not sacramental (miraculous), then the priest or bishop was just another layman whose profession it was to conduct church services and act as shepherd to the flock. And if Holy Orders conferred no miraculous powers, then the priest did nothing to the bread and wine, and the Mass became a mere ceremony memorializing the Last Supper. Take away Holy Orders and the church composed of ordained clergy is gone.

These ideas became the central core of the movement called Lollardy, which resembled a later movement, Lutheranism.

Whether Lollardy survived into the sixteenth century with sufficient strength to provide a direct link to, much less a cause of, Protestantism is still a subject of debate among scholars.

An example of Lollard anticlericalism, the denial of Holy Orders, was in fact not very widespread in England. There was a growing anticlericalism of another kind, however. The church's insistence that salvation came through the sacraments led to an exhaltation of the role and status of those who performed the sacraments. Members of the clergy were ordained in a miraculous ceremony and were thus empowered to work their miracles—the other sacraments. To be the "Lord's annointed" with the power to transform bread and wine into flesh and blood was to be truly set apart from the rest of the community. The rule of celibacy was a further sign of this special and unique status. The bishop was usually from a leading, if not noble, family and was thus socially removed from the people, even if he did appear among them on grand occasions and in a ceremonial state. Monks and nuns led cloistered lives; they were not usually seen by the laity and were honored from afar. The ordinary parish priest, however, was in a more vulnerable position. He was probably from one of the ordinary families in the area and grew up in the community. He continued to live among the people and work in the fields as they did; he drew his living from the glebe, farm land attached to the parish church. Other than being celibate, the priest was no different from his parishioners. They could observe and judge the level of his commitment to the church, his zeal in performing his duties, his rectitude, and the model of Christian living that he demonstrated. Because the lowly priest probably would never be promoted in the church hierarchy as a reward for devoted service, he had little professional incentive to rise much above the level of his fellow parishioners. It is not surprising that many priests were no more moral than their flock; what is surprising is how many of them were, in fact, committed churchmen. The laity was always of two minds about the clergy and their morals. If the priest truly honored his vows, he might be admired, but he also might be suspected of having secret vices. If the priest's morals were no better than those of the average person, he was subject to condemnation. The laity set higher standards for clergymen and attacked them whether or not they honored their vows. For priests and laymen, the sacraments and their (mechanical) performance were the truest signs of being a Christian.

Two of the rights enjoyed by the priests annoyed and occasionally enraged the laity. One was benefit of clergy, or the right of clergy to be tried in church court even for secular offenses. Over the centuries since the Norman Conquest, this right had been somewhat narrowed, although it still covered most criminal acts and it still defined as clergy anyone who could prove he was literate. The proof of literacy had in turn deteriorated to the point that the ability to quote a verse from the Bible sufficed. In England, Psalm 82:2, as we have seen, became known as the "hanging verse" because if one could recite it, one could literally get away with a murder. The other great annoyance was the right of a parish priest to a prescribed fee (mortuary) for burials and the probating of wills.

In addition to scholarly dispute about the long-range influence of the Lollards, there is an even greater dispute about the degree of anticlericalism in England prior to the Reformation. This dispute is itself part of the wider issue of the impulse behind the Reformation. All scholars agree that the English Reformation differed from the Reformation on the Continent. No one denies the central importance of Henry VIII's search for a divorce from Catherine of Aragon so that he could marry Anne Boleyn. The issue beyond this is whether Henry had to force his will upon a resistant populace or whether the country was ready when the time came. Scholarly agreement that the Reformation came to England from the top down has led to two conflicting interpretations: (1) that England was ready for the Reformation when the opportunity presented itself; and (2) that the king and his ministers forced it upon an unwilling, if not hostile, populace. Traditionally, Protestants have assumed that England was ready for the royal lead, that England was bound to be Protestant sooner or later. Catholics have assumed that Henry VIII was a tyrant who forced his will upon a reluctant people. (The fact that England eventually became a Protestant nation tends to be deemed irrelevant to our understanding of the first years of the Reformation.) These competing interpretations have led one side to attribute the inevitable Protestant victory to its origin in fourteenth-century Lollardy. The other side sees the development of a "Tudor despotism." More recent scholarship has taken long strides toward a reconciliation between the two opposing positions.

This new scholarship will be more fully developed later, but it can be briefly summarized now. According to Sir Geoffrey Elton, the Reformation did flow from the top down, but it did not require excessive force; Henry VIII was a law-abiding constitutional monarch. J. J. Scarisbrick insists that England was happy in its Catholic religion, that the Reformation was imposed by a tyrant, but that in the long run the Elizabethan Church of England did come to represent the true spirit of the English people and culture. Elton and Scarisbrick together give us a picture of a country that was largely content with its old religion; although the changes that were wrought came from on high, the final result was a country largely united in its new-found religion, which did, in fact, largely resemble the old religion in its fundamental forms, style, and structure. In their final analysis Henry VIII was a good Englishman and the English were good Anglicans! The story thus begins with the accession to the throne of Henry VIII in 1509.

2 / HENRY VIII AND THE BREAK

FROM ROME

Henry VIII acceded to the throne upon the death of his father, Henry VII, in 1509. Ever since the death of his older brother, Arthur, in 1502, Henry had been heir to the throne and had also been betrothed to his brother's widow, Catherine of Aragon. Henry VII had arranged for the marriage of Arthur and Catherine in a treaty with Ferdinand of Aragon in 1496. The young people were married in 1501, but Arthur died a few months later in 1502. Because the original treaty had been arranged for the mutual advantage of Spain and England, it was not particularly difficult to keep the alliance alive by forging a new marriage arrangement. However, marriage between Henry and Catherine was problematic because it was technically in violation of the canon law, which barred one from marrying a brother's widow. The papal power to bind (make rules) and to loose (dispense with the rules) had to be called upon. In 1503 Henry VII and Ferdinand had applied to Pope Julius II for a dispensation allowing the betrothal and marriage of Henry and Catherine. The dispensation had been granted, and Catherine had remained in England, as did her dowry, which had already been paid. Upon his accession, Henry VIII immediately did two things: he removed and had executed the closest advisers to his father, Empson and Dudley, and he married Catherine of Aragon. It was a love match as well as a diplomatic alliance, and enhanced Henry's great popularity even more: all the world loves a lover.

The young king and his bride had many things other than the dull routine of governmental administration to keep them busy. Henry was a fine and energetic athlete; a lover of music, both as performer and composer; a student of literature and theology; and a master of several foreign languages. His love of life and of his wife gave him the desire—and the inheritance of the greatest treasury in Western Europe gave him the freedom—to delegate much of the routine work of government to his ministers, one of whom was to become increasingly important and serve as a "lightning rod" that directed criticism away from the king himself.

Thomas Wolsey made himself indispensable to the king for many years, and he was handsomely rewarded for his services. As his power and rewards increased, so too did the dislike for him in the court and in the country. And the more he antagonized others, the more he needed the king's protection. Ever since the sixteenth century, there has been a debate among historians as to just how much power Wolsey actually had. Some have portrayed him as being all-powerful; others have been more willing to credit Henry with at least setting broad goals and then giving Wolsey the necessary control to implement them.

Thomas Wolsey, during his years of power (1509–1527), acquired through the king's efforts and his own a dominant position in both church and state. Each promotion in the church hierarchy did not mean that he relinquished the previous post; on the contrary, each new post was added on to the previous ones, resulting in ever-mounting income as well as increasing violations of the church ban on "pluralism," or the holding of more than one "living." His major offices were those of bishop of Lincoln and archbishop of York, which were acquired in 1514. The following year he became a cardinal in the Roman church and lord chancellor in the king's government. His annoyance at still being out-ranked in the church by the archbishop of Canterbury was assuaged in 1518 by the papal appointment as legate *a latere*. This title made him the equivalent of the pope in England on all topics of papal jurisdiction that the pope chose to delegate to him (annulments were not included). Wolsey had become through this vast accumulation of offices and revenues the living embodiment of the corruption that many saw as plaguing the church. All the evils of pluralism, simony (the purchase of church offices), nepotism, sexual unchastity, greed, and nonresidency (nonperformance) were there for all the world to see in the son of the Ipswich butcher. He also may have shown the very bright and ambitious young king that supreme power over church and state could in fact be combined in and exercised by one man. Wolsey had also shown that the proper application of the reformers' broom could result in the abolition of certain monasteries or chantries; their endowments could then be put to better use elsewhere. He used the confiscated endowments both to fill his own coffers and to endow Cardinal College at Oxford (the modern Christ Church College).

Wolsey and his like represented the "old learning"; the church of rules that could be dispensed with and rituals that could be performed by hired substitutes. The "new learning" that was spreading on the Continent provided an alternative sharp, critical analysis of the church's teachings and practices. The corruptions that Erasmus had so brilliantly described in *In Praise of Folly* clearly marked out the two roads the church could follow. Even though Erasmus himself remained loyal to the old church after the Lutheran reformation had begun, he presented an approach that gave credence and strength to those who would revert to a Lollard-like view of religion.

SECURING THE THRONE

Henry VIII was the first king since Richard II in 1377 to come to the throne with no challenge to his right to it. The Lancastrians who had succeeded Richard II had originally usurped the throne in 1399. Edward IV had seized it from the Lancastrian Henry IV in 1461; Richard III had probably committed murder in claiming the throne in 1483; and Henry VII had defeated Richard III at the Battle of Bosworth in 1485. The Wars of the Roses had gone on for another decade after that. The final removal of Lambert Simnel and Perkin Warbeck and their ill-starred rebellions in the 1490s had not necessarily guaranteed the end of the Wars of the Roses. Henry VII's decision to marry Elizabeth of York, the daughter of Edward IV, meant that the children of that union would have both Lancastrian and Yorkist blood in their veins. The stability that Henry VIII represented could be undone and the nation could once again be faced with dynastic warfare if Henry did not produce a legitimate heir. This issue was to become increasingly troublesome as the years passed. His only child by Catherine was a daughter, Mary. All the other pregnancies had resulted in miscarriages, stillbirths, or children who died in infancy. In a world where God was seen as the mover and instigator of every event (and every nonevent as well), the failure to provide an heir could be taken as a sign of divine displeasure. The lack of a male heir could result in a new War of the Roses.

As the years passed, Henry became more and more anxious about the succession and his love for Catherine waned. Throughout his marriage, he had expressed doubts about its validity, but always seemingly in a fit of anger. By 1527, however, Henry had come to a firm decision that the marriage was invalid according to God's law, if not the church's law. His decision to get a divorce, or an annulment in modern terms, was accompanied by an equally firm determination to marry Anne Boleyn, the daughter of a courtier and a relative of the powerful Howard family. The story of Henry VIII and Anne Boleyn has fascinated masses of people ever since. It is important to keep certain crucial facts in proper order in addressing "the king's great matter." Whether Henry desired Anne first and then sought a divorce or first wanted a divorce and then chose Anne is not really important. The basic fact is that Henry needed a male heir. Once Catherine had reached her forties (she was forty-one in 1527), she could no longer be seen as a potential bearer of an heir, even if the marriage were valid. Henry needed a new wife! Anne Boleyn was to be that wife and the mother of his heir. His daughter, Mary, would be put aside in favor of her hoped-for half-brother. Henry's reluctance to secure the throne for Mary was based upon the fact that the English crown had never gone to a woman; the one time that it had been tried, civil war was the result. Henry I's agreement with the nobility that his daughter Matilda would inherit the throne had not been honored. After nineteen years of civil war, Matilda's son, Henry of Anjou, defeated Stephen and became King Henry II a year later, upon Stephen's death. The precedent of Matilda and Stephen in 1135 should not be repeated.

Once Henry had decided on a divorce, he assigned Wolsey the task of getting it for him. Rather than let Wolsey, a lawyer, choose the grounds upon which to lodge the appeal, Henry chose them. He claimed that the law of God as given in Leviticus 20:21—"And if a man shall take his brother's wife, it is an unclean thing: he hath uncovered his brother's nakedness; they shall be childless"—was binding and could not be circumvented. Henry VIII had already demonstrated his command of theology, as well as his loyalty to the church, when he issued his *Assertio Septem Sacramentorum* (in Defense of the Seven Sacraments), which defended the seven sacraments and opposed the early attacks by Luther on the "good works" of the church. Henry considered himself to be equal, if not superior, to any theologian. Whether this claim was founded on his own ego or on theological grounds was to become an important issue later. Henry claimed that the laws of the church were of two origins: some existed because God wanted them; others existed because the church wanted them. It was Henry's position that the church could dispense with those laws that it had made, but not with those that God had made. Henry agreed that the Bible itself contained laws of both origins. How, then, was one to know which laws were which? Henry claimed that the historical tradition of the church supported his claim that Leviticus 20:21 was God's law. A young teacher at Cambridge University, Thomas Cranmer, suggested that church scholars throughout Europe be polled as to their views on Henry's interpretation. The poll was taken, and although the preponderance of views opposed Henry, there was enough scholarly support to lead the historian to conclude that Henry did have a case. The real issue, however, was not theological but political. Even though Henry lost the verdict of the scholars, he was determined to proceed on the same grounds, regardless. Since the publication of the magisterial biography of Henry by J. J. Scarisbrick[1] in 1968, historians have been aware that the story of the divorce was even more complex than had been traditionally thought. Cardinal Wolsey, with support within the Vatican, had found grounds for a divorce that might have been compelling. The Scarisbrick biography included a long chapter on the canon law of divorce that was based upon research in the Vatican archives as well as the English. To put the whole issue into focus will require close examination of the fine print in the papal dispensation and a sharp eye. How Henry re-

---

[1] J. J. Scarisbrick, *Henry VIII* (Berkeley and Los Angeles: University of California Press, 1968). Especially important is chapter VII, "The Canon Law of the Divorce," pp. 163–197.

sponded to Wolsey's discovery of a solution is of very great importance in trying to figure out just what Henry was after.

THE DIVORCE

According to canon law, a couple first had to be betrothed before being married; if the parties were not eligible to marry, they were also barred from being betrothed. Betrothal was just as binding as marriage and prevented either party from marrying anyone else as long as the betrothed lived, unless there were a papal dispensation. Once a betrothed couple was married, the marriage and the betrothal were merged into one legal state, assuming that the marriage had been complete, or consummated. When Henry VII and Ferdinand of Aragon had sought a dispensation from Pope Julius II authorizing the marriage of Catherine and Henry, the request left doubt as to whether the marriage of Catherine and Arthur had been consummated. The dispensation allowing the new marriage was equally vague. This lack of precision opened up opportunities for breaking the marriage of Catherine and Henry. During the long, bitter struggle for a divorce, Henry insisted that Catherine and Arthur had consummated their marriage; Catherine resolutely denied this. From Henry's point of view, the marriage of Catherine and Arthur had been consummated and the betrothal preceding it had therefore merged with the marriage. This put Henry on weak ground. The law was clear that if the marriage had been consummated, then a dispensation waiving that marriage was valid and the marriage of Catherine and Henry was valid. If Henry had only agreed with Catherine things would have been different. What really motivated Henry remains a mystery.

The dispensation granted by Pope Julius only included a waiver of the marriage between Catherine and Arthur, not their prior betrothal. Quite simply, it came down to the following alternatives: If Catherine had remained a virgin, then her betrothal to Arthur had not merged into her marriage to Arthur and the new dispensation allowing her to marry Henry by waiving her "marriage" to Arthur was invalid. What should have been waived was the betrothal. By insisting that she had consummated her marriage, Henry was actually undermining his own position. The only way for the new pope, Clement VII, to grant Henry his divorce would be to admit that Julius II had exceeded his power. No pope will do such a thing. By Clement VII agreeing with Catherine and accepting her virginity, the fault lay not with a pope who had exceeded his authority, but with two kings, Henry VII and Ferdinand, who had requested a dispensation on faulty grounds; Pope Julius had merely given them what they asked for. All Henry now had to do was to swallow his pride and admit that Catherine was right in proclaiming her virginity. Henry refused to do this. Why? That is the real question!

The very year, 1527, that Henry had sought his divorce saw the entry into and occupation of Rome by the forces of the Holy Roman emperor and king of Spain (Castille and Aragon), Charles V. Charles was the nephew of Catherine of Aragon and also a possible husband for Catherine's daughter, Mary Tudor. Charles had no intention of allowing the pope to grant Henry the divorce; the effects of an annulment would have been severe. By declaring that Catherine had never been married to Henry, Catherine would be put in the position of having been both a concubine and the mother of an illegitimate child. A proud and devout Spanish princess would not be so brutally treated as long as Charles could prevent it. Furthermore, illegitimacy for Mary would render her ineligible for a decent marriage of her own. She would be useless to Charles and any eventual merger of England and Spain would be blocked. So Clement VII, under pressure from the emperor, was in no position to grant a divorce unless the legal grounds were impeccable. Henry's own grounds were debatable at best. Wolsey, however, had shown the way: all Henry needed to do was to agree that Catherine had been a virgin and that the wrong dispensation had been acquired. There are several possible reasons for Henry's refusal to take advantage of the opportunities now available. One was that he was stubborn and wanted his own way; another possibility was that he had ceased to trust Wolsey, although Wolsey remained in office until after the disastrous trial at Blackfriars. The most plausible and intriguing possibility is that Henry had decided quite early in the whole process that he was going to get his divorce his way with or without the pope's consent. Perhaps he preferred not to have the pope's consent.

THE BREAK FROM ROME

Ever since William the Conqueror's settlement with the pope and the church after 1066, the king of England had a major, if not totally dominant, role in the staffing and administering of the church. In the reign of Edward I (1272–1307), a struggle ensued between the king and the pope over the right of the king to tax the clergy. The papal bull *Clericis Laicos* (1296) had prohibited the payment of money in any form or in any guise by the clergy to the laity. During the struggle, Edward I had declared "that England is in and of itself an empire." Thus, Edward was claiming to be in the same position relative to the church that any strong Holy Roman emperor had been. The imperial doctrine was that the emperor was the heir to the Caesars, who in turn had had the title *pontifex maximus* (high priest). All the power of an emperor Diocletian or a Constantine was claimed by the medieval emperors. If England were itself an empire, then Edward was an emperor, the *pontifex maximus*, the supreme ruler of church and state under God. Historians have known that Henry VIII revived the use of this claim by 1530 after the fall of Wolsey. J. J. Scarisbrick has stated that Henry was making this claim, or something similar, much earlier.[2] It may be that this claim to imperial (Roman) power was already motivating, if not dominating him. It is just possible that Henry all along was seeking total power, and the need for a divorce was just the opportunity to achieve supremacy in the English church. This "imperial" explanation has another facet to it: Henry was throughout his life a rival of Francis I of France. He waged war to conquer France before he sought his divorce; he would resume the effort after the Reformation. The rivalry was national, but it was also personal. Francis insisted that he, not Henry, was "the first gentleman of Europe." Within a year of acceding to the French throne, Francis had negotiated a treaty with the pope, the Concordat of Bologna in 1516, that gave him what any ambitious monarch would have dreamed of. For all practical purposes the king of France was supreme within the French church; he had effective royal supremacy with papal approval. Henry never sought to du-

---

2 J. J. Scarisbrick, *Henry VIII*, pp. 287–295.

plicate the papal agreement with France. Instead it is really quite possible that all along Henry VIII was actually trying to achieve that which he did in fact achieve in the end—the royal supremacy with the ties to Rome (Holy Roman Church and Holy Roman Empire) cut in twain.

Whatever may have been his motive, conscious or unconscious, the sequence of events is a story in its own right and has an inner logic. Whether this inner logic is merely the construct of the modern historian or the work of a masterly politician manipulating things according to a plan is a question we cannot answer.

The pope, obviously hoping to delay a decision for or against Henry's request, called for the establishment of a special court at Blackfriars in London. The court was jointly chaired by Cardinal Wolsey and the papal representative, Cardinal Campeggio. At the hearing, Catherine testified as to her virginity upon her marriage to Henry. Henry, in so many words, called her a liar. His once romantic passion for her had already become an intense hatred. Her refusal to agree with him led him to pray openly for her death. But praying for her death was as far as he would go. Whatever else one can say about Henry, he did not propose to remove her by illegal means. The papal instructions to Wolsey and Campeggio called for a decision. However, a set of secret instructions read on the eve of a decision called for the transferral of the court to Rome and a new beginning. Henry had lost this round, but Wolsey was to lose everything. Henry removed him from the lord chancellorship and sent him packing to his primatial see at York, which he had, in fact, never seen. Rumors of his negotiating with the king's enemies abroad resulted in his being summoned to stand trial in London. He died en route. In Wolsey's absence, Henry accused the whole body of the clergy of violating the Acts of *Praemunire* by having recognized Wolsey's legatine (or papal) authority against what was now the interest of the king.

Thomas More, until now a good friend of the king, was appointed lord chancellor, the first layman in a new tradition. Henry's even more momentous step was to call for a parliament. What became known as the "Reformation Parliament" met from 1529 to 1536, as momentous a span of years as any in England's history. Why a parliament was called is in itself an interesting matter. Normally, a parliament was called because the king needed money. The speech from the throne at the opening session would state the reasons the money was needed and the two houses could debate this and any other matters of interest. Once the king got his money, the parliament closed. This parliament was different! Henry had no special request to make. On the contrary, Henry seemed willing to let the members have some freedom to pursue topics of their own. This could be very dangerous for a king who was not in perfect rapport with those who sat in Parliament and those who had sent them. What this parliament wanted to talk about were the corruptions in the church. Anticlericalism, as has been said, did exist; whether or not it would have led to a reformation on its own is doubtful. But the timing was perfect for the king's interests. The more Parliament became worked up about the church, the more nervous the church became. The only one who could either agree to legislative attacks upon the church or to the vetoing of such bills was the king. The more upset Parliament was with the church, the more the church needed the king's protection. If this was Henry's goal, he was a clever politician. If this was not really a planned goal, then Henry was a lucky politician.

Early in Henry's reign, 1512, Parliament had restricted the right of benefit of clergy, excluding those in minor orders. In 1514 a murder in the Tower of London precipitated an outpouring of anticlerical rage. Richard Hunne had refused to pay the mortuary fee for the burial of his infant daughter. He was indicted by the church and responded with a charge of *praemunire*, claiming that the church courts represented a foreign authority. Hunne was arrested and sent to the Tower, where he was later found hanged. The church authorities claimed it was suicide and no action was taken against any possible villain. London was enraged. The memory of the Hunne affair had not yet died out when Henry called a parliament in 1529. Even though the first session lasted only six weeks, the tone of anticlericalism was set right from the start.

The fall of Wolsey had led to a temporary vacuum at the king's court. Thomas More had become lord chancellor, but he had a special agreement with the king that excused him from involvement in "the king's great matter." From the ranks of the deposed Wolsey's staff and from the benches in the House of Commons there soon emerged a man who would become almost as important to Henry and to history as Wolsey had been—Thomas Cromwell. As with Wolsey, so with Cromwell: what was the real relationship between the king and his chief minister?

Henry had called Parliament before Cromwell was entrenched. Did Cromwell merely carry out the royal program, or did Henry have no program beyond calling Parliament and had to wait for someone to tell him what to do? Sir Geoffrey Elton has devoted much of his spectacular career to the latter view, but not all historians agree. Because the policies were in the name of the king, we shall continue to refer to them as the king's policies and actions.

After two years of everything being "on hold," so to speak, with Anne Boleyn's father, the new ambassador to Rome, having no more success in Rome than Henry had allowed Wolsey to have, 1531 saw the beginning of action. Whether this was Cromwell's doing or Henry's really is not all that important. The English church's own equivalent of Parliament, Convocation, met to face the charge of *praemunire* for having recognized Wolsey's legatine authority. The clergy was now sufficiently frightened of Henry and/or Parliament that it responded with nearly total capitulation. Henry was recognized as being the "supreme head on earth of the Church in England, as far as the law of Christ allows." The "law of Christ" really refers to canon law and thus actually means nothing other than that the king is recognized has having the authority he was always recognized as having. The end result is, therefore, meaningless. As an earnest of their loyalty, the province of Canterbury awarded the king £100,000 and York offered £18,000. The king accepted the money and the title. The clergy was pardoned and the settlement was incorporated into an act of Parliament: the Act for the Submission of the Clergy. Some were heard to mutter that the king was now pope in England.

The pace now quickened. Cromwell quickly took a hand in writing legislation that struck out at the church. The House of Common's Supplication Against the Ordinaries in 1532 restricted the freedom to prosecute laymen charged with heresy and other offenses in the ecclesiastical courts. Henry specifically let it be known that he would no longer tolerate Convocation to meet without his having called it and that no new canons could be adopted in England without his approval. The supplication was followed by the death of William Warham, the archbishop of Canterbury, who had held office since 1503, blocking Wolsey and a host of others from the primatial see. The appointment of the right man at this moment could make all the difference. Henry knew his man—Thomas Cranmer, who had earlier advised him to consult the scholars of Europe. Cranmer was not a great figure as yet, but he was known to be a sincere churchman trying to make sense out of the increasingly conflicting theological views that were swirling around Cambridge. The king assumed Cranmer's absolute loyalty to the crown. His appointment would take time, however; the pope's approval was to be sought. With victory on the horizon for the king, Anne Boleyn was made marquis of Pembroke in her own right and after so many years of saying no, she consented to share the king's bed. The result was soon to be obvious. Sir Thomas More found his position to be beyond endurance and he resigned. More was later to deny the right of the king and the parliament to break the historic ties with the Roman church. The new chancellor would not be a factor in the story. Henry now increased the pressure on Rome by securing the passage of a statute that conditionally restrained the payment of annates (a bishop's first-year income) to Rome.

Cranmer's appointment was approved by the pope, although he probably knew as well as anyone what the future might bring. The pope, however, did not choose to stand in Henry's way on anything other than the "great matter" itself. Cranmer's position at Canterbury was now to be secured by the passage of the Act in Restraint of Appeals, which stopped all court cases from being appealed beyond Canterbury or York to Rome. Cranmer's archepiscopal court was now the only place to which a law-abiding king could seek a divorce. And Henry was indeed a law-abiding king, even if he had to create the laws that he would abide by. Henry now appealed to Cranmer for the dissolution of his marriage. The dissolution was granted in 1533 and Henry and Anne were soon married. Not long after that Anne was delivered of a baby girl—Elizabeth. All had been for nought! Henry was still without a male heir!

THE ROYAL SUPREMACY

Although the line of succession was still insecure, Henry continued to consolidate his power within and over the church. Even if this had not been his goal, he acted swiftly once the opportunity had been presented. The year 1534 was one of legislative activity that tied all the loose ends together. The cutoff of funds to Rome was completed with the passage of the Act of Annates and the abolition of Peter's Pence, the annual penny given by the laity to the pope. The abolition of annates was justified on the grounds of its financial burden (however, this "burden" did not prevent the king from soon ordering the payment of the annates to his own account). The annulment of the marriage to Catherine and the subsequent marriage to Anne, followed by the birth of Elizabeth, were buttressed by the passage of the Act of Succession in 1534. In English law the annulment and subsequent marriage were already legal, as was the legitimacy of Elizabeth. The purpose of the act was to make it a crime to deny these things. Henry had not been married to Catherine; Anne was his only wife; his daughter Mary was illegitimate, and Elizabeth was both legitimate and his only heir. To deny "in writing, print, deed, or act" the validity of the second marriage was high treason, punishable by death. To deny the marriage orally was a felony, punishable by imprisonment and loss of property. Henry hoped that his subjects would see this issue as a political litmus test for loyalty to the new order in church and state. The centerpiece of the new structure was the Act of Supremacy of 1534:

> Albeit the King's Majesty justly and rightfully is and oweth to be the supreme head of the Church of England, and so is recognized by the clergy of this realm in their Convocations; yet nevertheless for corroboration and confirmation thereof, and for increase of virtue in Christ's religion within this realm of England, and to repress and extirp all errors, heresies and other enormities and abuses heretofore used in the same. Be it enacted by authority of this present Parliament that the King our sovereign lord, his heirs and successors kings of this realm,

shall be taken, accepted and reputed the only supreme head in earth of the Church of England called *Anglicana Ecclesia,* and shall have and enjoy annexed and united to the imperial crown of this realm as well the title and style thereof, as all honours, dignities, preeminences, jurisdictions, privileges, authorities, immunities, profits and commodities, to the said dignity of supreme head of the same Church belonging and appertaining.[3]

The way the act was worded was significant and could be a cause of dispute in later years. From a strictly legal point of view, the act recognizes that the king is already supreme head; it does not make him so. From the point of view of Henry and all of his successors down to the Glorious Revolution, the king's authority is inherent in his "imperial" crown. All Parliament did was state what already was the case and make it a crime to deny it. In English law, the death penalty could not be used without a statutory authorization. The royal prerogative could assess fines, but nothing else. Magna Carta had prohibited the denial of life, liberty, or property without due process of law. "Due process of law" had been defined as being the common law back in the thirteenth century. The kings could always claim that Parliament had no real role in the church affairs other than to create punishable felonies. The future opponents of the kings could claim that Parliament had played an equal role in the Reformation and should have an equal voice in determining the role and structure of the church in the future. The seeds of conflict between crown and Parliament were being laid. Henry's use of Parliament was politically wise at the time; it gave Parliament future grounds for expanded claims. The king's official title was modified in 1535 to incorporate the words "Supreme Head of the Church of England," which succeeded the earlier papal designation "Defender of the Faith," which Henry and his successors have retained.

The break from Rome was complete. Once the ties with Rome were severed, the Church of England (or Anglican Church) was born. Where did England now stand? The Act of Supremacy outlined a vast array of rights that the kings had always had:

3 G. R. Elton, *The Tudor Constitution: Documents and Commentary* (Cambridge, Eng.: Cambridge University Press, 1968), p. 355.

...full power and authority from time to time to visit, repress, redress, reform, order, correct, restrain and amend all such errors, heresies, abuses, offences, contempts and enormities, whatsoever they be, which by any manner spiritual authority or jurisdiction ought or may lawfully be reformed, repressed, ordered, redressed, corrected, restrained or amended, most to the pleasure of Almighty God, the increase of virtue in Christ's religion, and for the conservation of the peace, unity and tranquility of this realm: any usage, custom, foreign laws, foreign authority, prescription of any other thing or things to the contrary notwithstanding.[4]

Taken at face value, the king's role was not in any way limited to that of a lay administrator. The right to "amend heresies," for instance, could at least imply that the king was the sole determiner of what was heresy and what was not. By amending heresies he was also creating new orthodoxy. The interpretation that Henry himself was to put upon all this was that he was himself a member of the clergy in his role as head of the church. In other words, he was the pope in England. The U.S. Constitution makes a civilian president the commander in chief of the armed forces. Henry VIII, however, claimed to be a clergyman over the church, not a layman. When Henry claimed to be an emperor, and when the Act of Supremacy referred to the "imperial crown," the reference goes back through the Holy Roman emperors to Constantine and the anti-Christian Diocletian before him. The Roman emperor was also the *pontifex maximus*, the high priest. Henry often came close to claiming this openly for himself; his actions were unquestionably in this vein. This link between political and religious powers was the system known as "Erastianism." Thomas Erastus, the sixteenth-century Swiss theologian, has been wrongly credited with supporting the supremacy of the state over the church.

Whether or not Henry VIII was a tyrant is partly a matter of how one defines tyranny. In an era in which there were no police and no standing army, tyranny in any modern sense was well nigh impossible without the cooperation of large and/or powerful forces within the wider society. It was Henry's hope that he

---

4 Elton, *Tudor Constitution*, p. 356.

could consolidate his new regime without resorting to force, which he did not have at his disposal, in any case. One way to establish his authority was to make examples of a few very prominent people; if he cracked down on a few of the right sort, perhaps a wider opposition could be scared off. It worked for a while. The two whom Henry chose for his examples were Sir Thomas More and Bishop Fisher of Rochester. The Act of Succession called for the swearing of an oath declaring that one believed that Princess Elizabeth was the sole heir to the throne. But the act also required the denial of Henry's marriage to Catherine and it implied a denial of papal supremacy. Fisher and More could agree to the first provision because Parliament had indeed enacted it into law. The second provision, however, required a denial of their deepest religious beliefs. Fisher had already that very year accepted the cardinal's hat from the pope. More did not deny that the Act of Succession had been properly enacted by a properly constituted parliament; however, he did deny that his or any other generation had the right to destroy the ties that bound the Christian community together throughout the world and throughout history. According to More, Parliament and the king together had exceeded their authority granted by God to humankind. More has been said to have died for conscience, but it is not that simple. More died for his own conscience, not for any old conscience. Having a conscience was not the issue; what your conscience said was the issue. The death of these two martyrs sent a shock wave through the country. Individual violations of the new regime were not to be a great problem after this. The Treason Act of 1534 gave the king added protection by including malicious talk along with malicious acts as being treasonable. This act could and did have a sweeping impact on potential critics of the new order.

THE CONSOLIDATION OF THE NEW ORDER

Thomas Cromwell organized the next steps in the consolidation of the new order. Henry needed money, and calling upon Parliament for its supply had proven to be difficult so far in Henry's reign. The lay dislike of the church's wealth, the carefully nurtured parliamentary anticlericalism, and the crown's skillful, if unscrupulous, exposure of corruption were all brought together in Cromwell's well-planned attack upon the monasteries. In late 1535, teams of investigators toured England's monasteries seeking evidence of corruption. They found plenty; they may have invented, or at least inflated, a good deal more. Some teams were able to cover more than one monastery per day, traveling some distance from one to the other. Honest or not, the "evidence" was damning. In February 1536, Cromwell got legislation calling for the closure of all monasteries with annual revenues of less than £200. The property was transferred to the crown. Because over the previous three centuries monasteries had used legal loopholes to put the title to their estates in the hands of laymen, Henry had struggled for some years and finally succeeded in 1535 in having the Statute of Uses enacted. This put the title in the name of the actual user, or beneficiary, of the property. The lands now legally belonged to the monasteries and Henry could confiscate them without directly attacking the laity. The confiscated property of 1536 was added to over the next four years by Cromwell's harrassing one large monastery after another into surrendering its property to the crown. The total value of the dissolved monasteries was sufficient to double the value of the crown lands. This was the greatest transfer of property since the Norman Conquest itself.

The use to which these lands and the revenues were put is another story. Much was sold quickly in a depressed market, much was given away in payment of previous debts, and much was given away as gifts. Some parcels remained in royal hands until the late seventeenth century. By the time Henry died in 1547, most of the land was gone, as were the proceeds. However, as damaging as this profligacy was for the crown, the fact that vast tracts of former church property were now in the hands of a large number of laymen created an influential class of people who may not have been persuaded by the theological truths of Protestantism, but they certainly were persuaded that these lands should never be restored to the church. All the new owners now had at least a limited financial interest in the new order in the English church.

The dissolution of the lesser monasteries coincided with the death by natural causes of Catherine of Aragon in 1536. Having been banished by Henry, she spent her last years under house arrest, rearing her "illegitimate" daughter, Mary, who grew up hating her father and all his works. Anne Boleyn also met her end in 1536, having failed to provide a son (and also perhaps because of derogatory comments about the king in bed). Henry accused her of adultery and she and the man accused with her were tried, convicted, and beheaded. Whether or not she had actually committed adultery will never be known, but if she were guilty she had to die: the Treason Act of 1352, which is still in effect, specifies that adultery by the queen consort and certain other royal ladies is treason. With the deaths of Catherine and Anne, Henry was free by legal or religious rules to remarry. Because he had had his marriage to Anne annulled before her execution, according to English law Henry had never been married and was the father of two illegitimate daughters. He still needed a legitimate male heir, and that meant that he needed to marry again and was at last truly free to do so. He chose Jane Seymour, with whom he fell in love. She was to give him his heir, Edward, although she was not to survive the ordeal of childbirth. The marriage to Jane emboldened Henry to take actions that would place his mark upon the Church of England. The diplomatic break between Spain and France, the two great Catholic powers, meant that he did not fear an imminent attack by either and could strike out on his own religiously. The result was the Ten Articles.

THE HENRICIAN CHURCH

The Ten Articles had been formulated by Convocation, with Cromwell's help. The substance and the wording were largely based upon the Wittenberg Articles composed by the Lutherans. That the "Defender of the Faith" who had denounced Luther some years previously should now be building his own structure upon a Lutheran foundation is proof of just how complex this whole era was and how complex a person Henry himself was. He began his life as a good Roman Catholic; he ended his life as a good Anglo-Catholic. In between he was many things and reached out in many directions. Was there a common denominator in all of this? Perhaps! But perhaps Henry was just letting the flowers bloom to see what came of it. The Ten Articles were clearly Lutheran. Only three of the seven sacraments were included: baptism, penance, and the Eucharist. In the section on the Eucharist, the "real presence" was accepted, rather than the full Lutheran formulation known as "consubstantiation." The "real presence" is a loosely defined acceptance that the body and blood of Christ are present. Whether this presence was in addition to or in place of the bread and wine was never made clear. The Ten retained auricular confession, unlike the Wittenberg Articles. Masses for the release of the souls of the dead from purgatory were denied, but purgatory itself was accepted, as were prayers for the dead. Wittenburg stressed salvation by faith; the Ten still added good works. The clergy were instructed to make the Ten Articles known to their flocks. As part of this new emphasis upon teaching, an order for the placing of an English Bible in every church was also issued. No Bible was available until 1539, however.

The fall of 1536 saw the outbreak of the only serious threat to Henry's rule, a revolt known as the Pilgrimage of Grace. The rebels likened themselves to pilgrims seeking to do the work of the Lord. The goals of the pilgrims and the treatment of those apprehended after the revolt was over tell us a great deal about the English and about Henry himself. The revolt began in Lincolnshire in early October and soon spread northward into Yorkshire and beyond. There were many issues involved, but at bottom it was a revolt against the new religion. The timing was directly linked to the dissolution of the monasteries in those remote regions of the north where the old medieval monastic traditions lived on. The north and west of England were sparsely settled, poor, and conservative culturally and socially. At the time of the dissolution, the monasteries were still serving as inns and hospitals, and the loyalties were still to the same families and the same ways of living. The dissolution was clearly the work of Thomas Cromwell, who was himself a newcomer to the power structure. The local clergy was concerned about its livelihood; the Ten Articles, with their elimination of four sacraments, could portend the loss of much more. It was not only a theological dispute that was raging; the issues carried the seeds of destruction for the north's way of life. The people fought back.

Robert Aske, a lawyer and a member of the gentry, was the principal leader in Yorkshire and was primarily motivated by religion. The rebels wanted the monasteries to be restored, the Statute of Uses to be repealed, and Thomas Cromwell and "heretical" bishops such as Cranmer to be dismissed. In fact, the rebels demanded that future councillors of the king should be established gentlemen, not newcomers like Cromwell (and Wolsey before him). All of these goals were to be achieved through the calling of a "true" or reformed parliament, free of royal control. In spite of this demand, there were no attacks upon the king himself or the dynasty. In fact, the rebels seemed to feel that Henry was, deep down, in agreement with them. He was not, but he lacked the force to crush them. The duke of Suffolk and later the duke of Norfolk provided the armed forces to put down the rebels before they could move south and threaten the government on its own territory. That the king had to call upon the armed forces of one of his own subjects shows how lacking in force he was.

Calling upon the Norfolk forces was a throwback to the anarchy of the Wars of the Roses. Henry and his father before him had tried to eliminate private armies altogether. Dependence upon Norfolk or any other subject raised the specter of the "overmighty subject" and all the horrors of anarchy and civil war that that could produce. Norfolk crushed the rebels and set about a bloody pacification. About 250 were executed after a trial of some sort; many, however, were tried and acquitted, even after the king had urged the local juries to find the rebels guilty. That juries defied the royal admonitions and that they got away with doing so can be used as evidence that Henry's rule was far from being as tyrannical as the "Tudor despotism" school of historians would like to think.

In an effort to present the nation with a clear statement of the theological content of the new religious order, Cranmer and his episcopal colleagues issued in 1537 *The Godly and Pious Institution of a Christian Man*, commonly called the Bishops' Book. This document had a strong Lutheran element, and the numerous marginal notes added by Henry himself confuse the issues as much as they clarify them. The Bishops' Book did restore the four missing sacraments from the Ten Articles, but listed as the "greater" sacraments baptism, penance, and Eucharist. Henry in his marginal notes transferred matrimony from the "lesser" category to the "greater." There can be no doubt about Henry's commitment to the blessed state of matrimony (after all, he had six wives, not six mistresses). The discussion of the Eucharist was not anti-Catholic, but the words used were not the traditional Catholic ones, either. The word Mass rarely appeared in the document, and among the functions of a clergyman there was no mention of the sacrifice of the altar. In fact, the Bishops' Book limits the priest's function to teaching and preaching and makes no distinction between the role of the bishop and that of the priest. This was all very Protestant, and Henry's marginal notes did not change this. Also in his notes, Henry largely removed any meaning left with the sacrament of confirmation. He saw it as no more than an illumination of the benefits bestowed by the four "real" sacraments. Wycliffe had taken the same stand in the fourteenth century. The selective use of deletions effectively removed any particular significance from the sacrament of Extreme Unction as well. The overall tone of Henry's changes was in the Lutheran direction. The way in which he dealt with the sacrament of Holy Orders was to be distinctly Henrician, however, and may be the key to opening the door into his real motives.

Traditionally, the "ordering" of bishops was in two steps, the selection of the man and the conferring upon him of his status. The Bishops' Book said that in ancient times the apostles were to "elect, call, and admit" their successors. Henry commented on this by saying that in ancient times there were no Christian kings. This could mean that now that there were Christian kings, the sole and complete power to order the clergy resided with the king, not the successors to the apostles. In later years and in other writings the king's true intent was made even clearer. Henry does seem to intend that the Christian king, or at least one such king, creates a bishop by the mere act of appointing him. If this is what Henry meant, then he was indeed claiming to be a Holy Roman emperor and a pope all wrapped into one. The bishops themselves had already offered him the opportunity to make grand claims by having stated in the Bishops' Book that "without the...power and license of your majesty we knowledge and confess that we have none authority."

Without the fear of immediate attack upon England from any Catholic quarter, Henry may have been indulging his own religious desires. It is doubtful that a man as keenly interested in and knowledgeable about religion as he would merely be directed by Cromwell, Cranmer, or any other courtier. What we see is probably the product of Henry's own heart and mind. If so, it is worth exploring his marginal notes a bit further. What we see is a man for whom the faith by which alone a person is saved according to the Protestant tradition is nothing more than an intellectual acceptance of certain words. He stresses that salvation requires the living of a good Christian life, but he does not see these "good works" as being in the sacraments of the church. By stressing something more than faith, he was taking a non-Protestant view; by reordering and downplaying the sacraments, he was taking a non-Catholic view. By considering faith to be a prescribed formula rather than an emotional, soul-wrenching oneness with God, Henry was not really religious in any way that the theologians of the sixteenth century were religious. In a nutshell, what Henry was saying was that it was the duty of man to obey his Christian prince. "The powers that be, they are ordained of God." The Christian prince and his laws were seen as substitutes for the saints and the clergy. Henry said Christians should pray directly to Christ and not through the saints or to the Father. Between Jesus Christ and the mortal Christian was nothing but the king. This was neither Protestantism nor Catholicism. This was the Henrician Church of England!

The year 1537 drew to a close with the birth of the long-desired and prayed-for legitimate son and heir, Prince Edward. The birth was a difficult one for Queen Jane Seymour. When Henry would postpone the baptism no longer, she left her bed, attended the ceremony, hemorrhaged, and died. Once again Henry was without a wife, but he did have his heir and did not, therefore, have any pressing need for another wife. However, in those days of high mortality of infants and children, one son was not a guarantee of a male heir. The newly achieved tranquility was not to last for long.

During the summer of 1538, France and Spain completed several months of negotiations and agreed to the Peace of Nice. Peace between the two great Catholic powers held grave consequences for England. Henry's own religious inclinations were already outlined. Cromwell, probably because of his beliefs, and certainly for strategic reasons, sought to have England move in a more Protestant direction and actually seek a Protestant alliance in Europe. Henry was not inclined to take the Lutheran route unless the benefits were very real. Cromwell issued a set of injunctions declaring war on "popish and superstitious practices," among which were pilgrimages to the tomb of St. Thomas Becket at Canterbury. Cromwell had the tomb destroyed and the endowment transferred to the crown. The benefits were real indeed! But the Injunctions of 1538 were additions to the earlier Injunctions of 1536 and were modified by the king.

Cromwell, on behalf of the king, had assumed the role of "visitor" to the clergy, a role traditionally played by the bishop of a diocese. Upon concluding a "visitation," the bishop would issue "injunctions" mandating whatever corrections the visit found to be necessary. The first Injunctions of 1536 were of a reforming nature, even Erasmian; they established that the role of the clergy was to teach and preach, enforce the moral laws, and encourage the giving of alms. The second set of injunctions had continued in this same vein, with added attack upon pilgrimages and images, as we have just seen. The overall Protestant tone of what were undoubtedly Cromwell's injunctions was quickly cast aside by the king's own proclamation of 1538 against "Diversities in Religion," ostensibly intended to enforce the injunctions. Henry's proclamation gives us a real clue as to just what he himself thought about it all.

Professor Elton has summed up the significance of the proclamation with great candor and clarity: "they [the injunctions] display his reluctance to go further in the direction of reform and also his characteristic leaning to Savagery."[5] The ten points of the proclamation can be briefly summarized:

---

5 G. R. Elton, *Policy and Police: The Enforcement of the Reformation in the Age of Thomas Cromwell* (Cambridge, Eng.: Cambridge University Press, 1972), pp. 255–56.

1. The importation of English books was forbidden without a special license.
2. All printing was now to be licensed by the Privy Council and any hint of royal approval of the contents had to be verified by an imprimatur.
3. All Bibles must have any prefaces and/or notes approved by the king or the Privy Council.
4. Only authorized versions of the Bible could be sold.
5. Anabaptists and other "enemies" of the sacraments were to be executed or expelled.
6. Discussion of the meaning of the Eucharist was forbidden.
7. All rites not specifically abolished were to be observed. (Many had been ignored because of attacks upon "superstition.")
8. Clerical celibacy was restored, with marriage of the clergy condemned as contrary to Scripture and the early church fathers.
9. "False superstitions" were to be combatted by better teaching.
10. Thomas Becket and all his works were condemned.

The last two points seem once again to reflect Cromwell's views and were, in fact, added separately. But, as we saw, Henry benefited financially from the attack on Becket, and, of course, what Becket stood for in the twelfth century was directly counter to everything Henry stood for now, and perhaps much earlier in his reign as well.

The proclamation was undoubtedly the work of Henry himself. The struggle at court was not over, however. In 1539 a new proclamation soon appeared that seems to be the work of Cranmer and Cromwell. The new one stressed that the restored ceremonies were only to be "aids" to contemplation, not necessary means to salvation, and also pardoned the Anabaptists. The conflicts at court between Henry and Cromwell, allied with Cranmer, were soon to reach a height of great danger for at least one of the participants and great annoyance for another. Cromwell was continuing to push for the Protestant alliance on the Continent, while Henry was trying to mold a church that would meet his own requirements.

The religious disputes were linked, of course, with the grander diplomatic strategy. Cromwell, who was quite comfortable with

Lutheran ideas and practices, sought a Protestant basis in England as an earnest of a Protestant alliance on the Continent. To Henry's mind, and that was a mind fully accepting of much of Catholicism anyway, the better way to defend England from a Catholic attack was to appear to be moving back into a Catholic mold. Why should Spain and/or France go to war if Henry were already moving their way? Cromwell was in the driver's seat at first.

England pursued an alliance with Cleves, a small German state in opposition to Charles V, and the price that Henry would have to pay for such an alliance was marriage to Anne of Cleves, the duke's daughter. It was unusual for a high-born woman of twenty-five to be unmarried, and Henry wondered what was wrong with Anne. Cromwell had Holbein paint her portrait. Henry accepted both the portrait (which was excessively flattering) and the woman. Henry was furious when he finally saw her; although he married her officially, he sought deliverance from her and from Cromwell. (Holbein was lucky that Henry did not seek revenge on him also.) The alliance and subsequent marriage had been a victory, albeit a Pyrrhic one, for Cromwell. The religious victory had gone to the king even before Anne's arrival. Henry could now enact his own religious settlement.

THE ACT OF SIX ARTICLES

The Act of Six Articles had been pushed through Parliament in 1539 against the wishes of Cromwell and Cranmer, with the support of the Howards, who were Catholic. The Act for Abolishing the Diversities of Opinion (or the Six Articles or the "whip with six strings") proclaimed the doctrine of transubstantiation; required auricular confession; and affirmed the sanctity of monastic vows (no irony intended, one hopes); the continuation of communion in one kind (bread) for the laity; the efficacy of private masses; and clerical celibacy. This was Roman Catholicism, pure and simple. Henry had strengthened the church's position on celibacy by declaring that it was God's will, not just a matter of church discipline. Henry was once again demonstrating that he alone could discern the will of God. The Act of Six Articles also served as a statute against heresy, and in effect converted heresy from an ecclesiastical offense to a common-law offense. An additional statute of 1543 called for the indictment of offenders cited on the oath of twelve commissioners appointed by the crown. The penalty for denial of transubstantiation was burning at the stake; violations of the other five articles resulted in hanging after a second offense. The doctrines of the Church of England were now in the hands of the king—not the king-in-parliament, but the king alone. The church was now a branch of the state and the state was the king, allied with and in tune with God.

Henry's annoyance over the marriage with Anne of Cleves spelled disaster for Cromwell. Relations between France and Spain were already souring, reducing the chance that either would attack England. Stephen Gardiner, the conservative bishop of Winchester, had served as ambassador in Paris and prepared the way for French-English friendship if Cromwell were removed from office. The alliance, and the accompanying marriage that Cromwell had arranged for Henry, were doomed. The ultimate price was to be paid by Cromwell himself. The duke of Norfolk was already conspiring to have Henry become enamored of his niece, Catherine Howard. All the Howards were to remain Catholic, or at least were to lean to the Catholic side of issues. The marriage to Anne of Cleves would have to be annulled. Cromwell fought to save himself, even arranging to have himself ennobled with the title earl of Essex. However, all was to no avail. In the summer of 1540 he was condemned to death for both treason and heresy by an act of attainder. Guilty of neither, he declared his devotion to the true Catholic faith as he met his end. He may have been no heretic, but he surely was no Catholic, either. He and Cranmer were increasingly in tune with what were Protestant opinions coming into England from the Continent.

THE LAST YEARS OF HENRY'S REIGN

The last years of Henry's reign were without question the years where Henry alone made the big decisions. Historians debate the extent to which Henry was dependent upon Cardinal Wolsey and Thomas Cromwell. The last seven years of the reign saw no one minister emerge with anything like the same claim to influence. For good or ill, Henry was the master of his own fate. Cromwell's fall was followed by marriage to Catherine Howard and one more attempt at marital bliss, and perhaps an additional heir. Religiously, the new era also quickly saw the triumph of Catholicism without the pope. The marriage to Catherine was not to last; she was found guilty of a fall from chastity prior to marrying Henry and sentenced to death. The return of full-blown Catholicism persisted to the end of the reign.

The King's Book, or the *Necessary Doctrine and Erudition for Christian Man,* was published in 1543 in conjunction with an act of Parliament that quite completely put *finis* to the reform movement. The king himself wrote the preface and made some revisions to the bishops' draft. The King's Book came down firmly on the side of salvation by faith and good works, as opposed to the Protestants' exclusive reliance upon faith. This was indeed the crucial distinction between Catholic and Protestant, as the great humanist Erasmus had early declared when he refused to become a Lutheran. It was, and is, upon this issue that so much of the great controversies within our Western Civilization depend. The Lutheran and Calvinist stress upon faith, which faith was in turn the gift of God bestowed prior to birth (predestination), exalted the sovereignty of God and denied any voice in one's own salvation to the human being. The Catholic position on faith and good works offered a voice to the human being, however small or large that voice might be. If human beings had some input into their own salvation, it was then the Catholic system that was "humanist," not the Protestant. It also, of course, meant that the sacraments and the clergy who performed those sacraments had special roles to play and had, in fact, a hold over their fellow human beings. The king's variation on this grand and crucial theme was that the king who appointed the clergy was himself the representative of God on earth, or at least in England. Just what Henry was now claiming on this score must be examined in greater detail. It is here that the unique status of the Church of England rests.

The powers enjoyed and exercised by those in authority in the Catholic tradition are of two kinds: *potestas gladii* and *potestas ordinis.* The former refers to the civil power and governance granted to kings and princes by Christ; the latter refers to the priestly powers. These are the two swords of medieval tradition: the secular or temporal sword and the spiritual or ecclesiastical sword. Catholic tradition distinguished between the two, with the spiritual always considered to be superior, at least in the last analysis. From this came the pope's claim to supremacy over kings and other magistrates. The tradition of the Holy Roman emperors was the claim of temporal superiority over the spiritual, at least as regards the emperor. This was what the phase "England is in and of itself an Empire" referred to when used by Edward I and more recently by Henry VIII, as we have seen above. What Henry was now claiming was a new twist on the old imperial refrain.

The power to appoint bishops had been thoroughly established as a royal prerogative both by long usage and by papal agreement following the various investiture controversies in the Middle Ages. The Bishops' Book of 1537 had clearly stated that "we may not think that it doth appertain unto the office of kings and princes to preach and teach, to administer the sacraments, to absolve, to excommunicate, and such others things belonging to the office and administration of bishops and priests." Henry had seen fit to add at this point another marginal note: "the laws of every region" must rule, however. (What did this mean?)

What Henry meant may be made clearer by continuing the chronological survey. The Six Articles was followed by the creation of a commission of inquiry that issued seventeen interrogatories to the bishops. Six of the questions concerned ordination. Henry wondered why only bishops could perform the sacrament of ordination. Cranmer said that in emergencies the king or prince could create priests and bishops. Cranmer also said the king was responsible for the "cure of souls," although it seemed that he meant jurisdictional responsibility, not the commission of personal acts. The King's Book itself dropped the distinction between the *potestas gladii* and the *potestas ordinis*. The King's Book also dropped the denial of the royal cure of souls that had appeared in the Bishops' Book. Does this imply something? Perhaps. Professor Leo Solt said it created opportunity for greater reform later, but he did not make it clear just what kind of reform he had in mind. Professor Scarisbrick said that the basic theme underlying the whole Henrician religious corpus was anticlericalism, an anticlericalism that often, but not necessarily always, resulted in the substitution of the king for the clergy.

The Henrician religious "settlement" (if we can call it that) was essentially Catholic as far as the man in the street (or in the pew) could tell. The Pilgrimage of Grace had already shown that the mass of people were quite conservative and quite determined to hold on to their traditional ways. That Henry had accomplished: Mass was still said by the same clergy, with the same liturgy, and the need for auricular confession was retained. The disputes over the *potestas gladii* versus the *potestas ordinis* did not reach the level of ordinary people; it was a dispute among a handful of leaders at the top. The only real change had been the dissolution of the monasteries, and that in turn had produced the only real rebellion. The first steps had also been taken to secularize some of the role that the monasteries had traditionally played. The Beggars Act of 1536 allowed the licensing of worthy beggars and was the first, albeit short-lived, step at "nationalizing" the problem of welfare for the poor. The first steps on the way to the full-blown Elizabethan Poor Law system had been taken.

The break from Rome was a truly revolutionary act in its own right, regardless of all the other changes that would eventually come in its wake. This break was imposed from on high. The king, and/or his ministers, made use of a representative parliament which reflected a high degree of native anticlericalism. This anticlericalism was used by the crown to frighten the churchmen individually, and through the collectivity of Convocation they were frightened into supporting Henry out of fear of that very parliament. The anticlericalism was also allied with an emergent English nationalism that could be turned into antiforeign sentiment. The break from Rome was indeed a break from all things Roman, church and empire. It would lead to a deep insularity and even xenophobia before the close of the sixteenth century. By declaring equality with the Holy Roman emperors, Henry was also declaring independence from all things Roman, Catholic, Continental. Sir Thomas More understood all of this. That is why he chose to die!

As the reign drew to a close, the archbishop of Canterbury, Thomas Cranmer, and the last of Henry's queens, Catherine Parr, were the only ones who could discuss religion with Henry, challenge him, and survive. For Cranmer, the royal supremacy was a true article of faith; on all other matters of religion he was moving slowly but surely towards Protestantism. His profound loyalty to the royal supremacy was surely seen by Henry and made the king feel secure; although Cranmer might disagree with Henry, nothing of consequence would come of it. Henry had the same assurance in his relationship with Catherine Parr.

How and why Henry arranged for the governance of the realm in his young son's reign is still something of a mystery, but perhaps there is a key. By 1547, Henry must have known that he would not live to see young Edward reach his majority, and he made provisions. He appointed a Council of State whose members all were identified as supporters of the Protestant reform movement. Why would the king who had just imposed the Six Articles and the King's Book upon the nation now place the supreme power in a council that did not include any of the known Catholic sympathizers? Edward and his sister Elizabeth had both been raised by tutors of a reforming bent and with the influence of Anne of Cleves. Because Henry had used his last years in power to spend his new-found ecclesiastical fortune in a vain attempt to conquer France, as any red-blooded medieval king would wish to do, he needed to secure the future defense of England. His councillors not only were sympathetic to religious reform but also were men of experience in the military or the naval forces. Perhaps this factor carried greater weight than the religious one.

Provision had also been made for the succession beyond Edward, who was not overly robust. Henry had been authorized by an act of Parliament to specify the succession in his will. The result was a mixture of a father's acceptance of his own children and of an Englishman's fear of the Scots. After Henry came Edward and his heirs. Then came his elder daughter, Mary (Catholic or not), and her heirs. Next was the younger daughter, Elizabeth (Protestant or not), and her heirs. So far the rules of biological order had prevailed. This was to be changed if Elizabeth had no heirs. Instead of the crown going to the descendants of Henry's sister Margaret, who had married James IV of Scotland, Henry called for the crown to go first to the descendants of his younger sister, Mary, who had married Charles Brandon, duke of Suffolk, an Englishman. So Henry died with the line of succession being in the traditional birth order for his own children but with an adjustment made to prevent the union of England and Scotland. The council of military men, sympathetic to reform, was not to give way to any one great individual leader. Edward Seymour and John Dudley had their own plans, and time was on their side. Nevertheless, the death of Henry VIII in 1547 marked the end of an era, just as his life had put an indelible mark upon England and its place in the European order.

3 / THE LITTLE TUDORS:
EDWARD VI AND MARY I

LORD PROTECTOR SOMERSET

The new king was a boy of ten, bright, even precocious, and interested to the point of bigotry in religion. The English constitution had never evolved a real role for a minor on the throne; there was no common-law rule for a regency. In theory, Edward VI was king and that was that. The initial oaths of allegiance were sworn to the "King, Supreme Head, and Defender of the Faith." Some later on were to question whether or not a child could be supreme head of the church. This very questioning of his status was another implication that the office of supreme head was within the clergy, not outside it. Edward's already developing views on religion were definitely in the reform tradition. We can quite safely say that Edward VI was a Protestant; so was his uncle Seymour, who quickly put aside the special rules left behind by Henry VIII and became a one-man ruler, taking the titles of duke of Somerset and lord protector. Somerset moved fast to secure his own power and then to put the new reign on a new religious footing. Archbishop Cranmer was intellectually and spiritually ready to assist the lord protector and the king in establishing the new regime. Somerset supported the new religious system, but he would prove to be incapable of giving it the forceful backing it required in order to maintain peace in the realm. Whether Somerset's lack of decisiveness resulted from a highly developed sense of toleration or was mere weakness is still a matter of controversy.

Within a month of Henry's death, Cranmer issued a set of injunctions calling for the introduction of some new books, composed in English by Cranmer himself, for use in the litany and other prayer services. Among the most important was the Book of Homilies or sermons ready-made for use in churches. One of those, composed by Cranmer himself, dealt with Christian obedience: kings must be obeyed "though they be wicked and wrong doers." If a command was against the word of God, then it was not to be obeyed; however, "we may not in any wise withstand violently, or rebel against rulers, or make any insurrection, sedition, or tumults, either by force of arms or otherwise . . . but . . . patiently suffer all wrongs, and injuries."

The principal act that could be seen as an example of toleration was the Act of Repeal of 1547, which was passed on Parliament's own initiative. This act repealed the Henrician heresy laws, along with the Six Articles and the Henrician Treason Act; it retained the pre-Henrician laws against heresy and treason. Heretics could still be burned at the stake, and some still were. Another act in 1547 actually strengthened the king's role in the selection of bishops, eliminating even the fiction that an election was needed to confirm the royal appointment: ". . . all authority of Jurisdiction, Spiritual and Temporal, is derived and deducted from the King's Majesty, as supreme head. . . ." It also declared that the "Courts Ecclesiastical . . . be kept by no other power, or authority, either foreign or within the Realm" except the royal power. The new religious settlement was completed with another statute in 1547 that dissolved the chantries, which had been private foundations, endowed over the centuries for religious, charitable, or educational purposes. Much of the endowment in the form of land had come from the newly emerging gentry and business classes of the later Middle Ages. The funds' recipients were priests who were paid to say masses around the clock for the souls of the departed designated by the donors. The charitable and educational work affected large numbers of laity, and the total effect upon society of the chantries' dissolution was perhaps even greater than that of the dissolution of the monasteries. The royal coffers were once again given a shot in the arm, and once again the money disappeared all too quicky. Somerset himself acquired several choice pieces. (Henry VIII is attacked for squandering the proceeds from the monasteries; no one receives any particular blame for the squandering of the chantry proceeds). The dissolution of the chantries also put an end to many masses for the dead. This was a step along the reforming road away from belief in purgatory. The authorization for the taking of communion in two kinds by the laity was also a step in the reformers' direction and completed a busy first session of Edward's first parliament.

THOMAS CRANMER
AND THE FIRST PRAYER BOOKS

The man who would soon take center stage as the chief reformer was the archbishop of Canterbury himself, Thomas Cranmer. The first acts of the reign were in his mold: strengthening the role of the king while also making the liturgy and the doctrines it symbolized more Protestant. Cranmer's rise was countered by the removal from office of Stephen Gardiner, the bishop of Winchester, who had appeared to be the dominant figure in the last days of Henry's reign. Cranmer was essentially a scholar, not a politician. But, even more, he was a man of deep religious convictions for which he was willing to die, if need be. Unlike many others who can be called martyrs, Cranmer did not have a fixed set of beliefs to which he adhered from beginning to end.

Cranmer's scholarly pursuit of inquiry was genuine, but the inquiry was both intellectually and religiously (or spiritually) based. At each step in the development of his understanding he truly believed in the particular beliefs associated with that step. As he moved on intellectually, so he moved on spiritually. Because he himself was aware of his own personal religious development, he could understand and accept that others might be at a different stage in their own religious life. To that extent he was able to tolerate the differing views of others and to accept that the king's views took precedence over his own. In any case, one of Cranmer's fundamental beliefs was the belief in the royal supremacy. He could disagree with Henry and submit in the end without being untrue to himself. Henry could accept disagreements with Cranmer, because Henry knew that Cranmer, at bottom, was loyal. Once Catholic Mary came to the throne, Cranmer would find that his belief in the royal supremacy was at odds with his Protestant faith. The conflict was painful, but so was being burned at the stake. In the end he put the reformed faith ahead of the royal supremacy; it is very important to keep that end in mind when looking at the work that Cranmer wrought during Edward's reign.

However easy it is to see the political and religious compromises that Cranmer's prayer books demonstrated, the fact is that they represented his mature and sincerely held beliefs. Cranmer is often remembered for his magnificent use of the English language and for his ability to fudge great doctrinal issues. He was also a man of deep faith who gave his life for his beliefs; he was just as much a martyr as Thomas More. Unlike More, however, Cranmer is more often remembered for his temporary recantation than for his final decision to die. He was actually less a "man for all seasons" than More. His legacy is probably a greater one, all told.

By 1549 Cranmer had completed work on his first prayer book, the Book of Common Prayer. The timing of its appearance was significant. Cranmer had benefited from the ending of the attack upon Protestantism and had been able to buttress his religious views with those brought into England by a new wave of Protestant religious thinkers from the Continent, among whom were John a Lasco from Poland, Martin Bucer from Strasbourg, Francis Dryander (Francisco de Encinas) from Spain, and Peter Martyr (Pietro Martire Vermigli) from Italy. Their combined influence created an atmosphere in which Cranmer could move forward intellectually. As we shall see, he was not, as yet, to move as far or as fast as they wanted or expected. Whatever other influences there may have been on Cranmer, the greatest were the Bible and his own intellectual and spiritual understanding of what it meant for the present and the future, as well as in the past. For Cranmer, as for anyone else who was led to challenge the teachings and practices of the historic Catholic church, some locus of authority greater than the Catholic church had to be identified. That point of authority could only be the Bible. The only other possible alternative was the claim to a personal divine relevation (there were some, especially on the Continent, who did make such claims). In both the short and the long run, any claims to revelations were of little influence except upon the life of some revered individuals. Cranmer wrote in the preface to the 1549 book:

that all the Bible should be read over once in the year, intending thereby, that the Clergy, and especially such as were Ministers of the congregation, should (by often reading and mediation of Gods word) be stirred up to godliness themselves, and be more able also to exhorte others by wholesome doctrine, and to confute them that were adversaries to the truth.

The title, Book of Common Prayer, was derived from the same use of the word "common" as in the term "common law." Prior to Cranmer's 1549 book, there was no one prayer book. The Catholic clergyman had the various services or parts of the liturgy available in his own hand or in print. A bishop who might have to conduct a variety of services would have to carry around with him a bag of books. All were in Latin. The central service, the Mass, was performed somewhat differently in different dioceses. There was no one standard liturgy; there was no one book in which to find everything. In the basic sense, what Cranmer did was to translate the Latin into English, choose one form of liturgy where there was variety, and then to put it all between one set of covers. In the process of choosing the particular style of liturgy and in the actual act of translating from Latin into English, he could make changes, minor or major, if and when he desired. Did he make changes from the Latin originals to stake out a new position on doctrine or to fudge the differences between the Catholic and Protestant canons? That Cranmer's Prayer Book was a *via media* (middle way) is accepted. To what extent the via media is the result of honest theology or of a deliberate act of compromise has always been an issue. Most scholars today would credit Cranmer with intellectual and theological honesty. The Elizabethan Prayer Book of 1559 (a later variation) may be another matter. The words of A. G. Dickens are probably as good a summary as we can get:

> Though wholly in the English language, this Prayer Book remained a masterpiece of compromise, even of studied ambiguity. While it did not specifically deny Catholic doctrine, its ambiguous phrases were understood by its author in a Protestant sense and intended to enable Protestants to use it with a good conscience.[1]

---

1 A. G. Dickens, *The English Reformation* (London: Batsford, 1964), p. 219.

Why was there a need for a compromise at all? If the king and the lord protector were both Protestants and if Cranmer himself was certainly already a Protestant as well, why not do the Protestant thing and get it over with? As has been seen from the beginning of the story, the English Reformation was an act of state, imposed from above upon a nation that may have been willing to accept it, but that had not itself sought to experience such a reformation. Cranmer's ambivalence was itself a very real reflection of the ambivalence within the nation. It is not so much that Cranmer sought to be ambiguous, but that he was sincerely ambiguous and was therefore a true microcosm of the nation at large. Cranmer and his Prayer Books were at the center of English religious life for four hundred years because they were truly representative of the English nation, or at least a large majority of the nation. The magnificent style added to the potent force, but did not create it. The compromise was not imposed from on high; it was inspired on high and given to a largely receptive nation. The Catholic revival of the next reign and the centuries of Puritan, dissenting, and nonconformist opposition movements do not detract from the fact that the English people at heart are Church of England or they are nothing. (Currently, "nothing" seems to be dominant.)

Just what was this compromise? If we turn first to what might be seen as the political imperative, we see an England in which the great mass of the people were illiterate, or nearly so. Literate or not, the great mass certainly had never read the theological tracts of the continental reformers, or those of their English followers. The disputes over Catholic versus Protestant theological issues were of consequence for scholars at the universities, some of the more intellectually inclined clergy, and some of the educated, or at least literate, members of the urban middle and upper classes who traveled abroad, met those who traveled abroad, or consorted with foreigners residing in London and other urban centers. For these people, there were real doctrinal issues to think about, and to fight about. For the great mass of the population, however, urban as well as rural, the traditional religion was part and parcel of their way of life. It was accepted along with the seasons of the year, which the church calendar in fact mirrored. One might or might not like the parish priest. One might or might not like the payment of money to that priest. The people did not like corruption, nor did they usually like lord bishops acting too lordly. The educated might grumble about the lack of good sermons, or even the lack of the sermon itself, good or bad. The ordinary parishioner never put much stock in sermons anyway. It was the mystery of the Mass and the other sacraments that made one feel that one had met God. The average person was not an intellectual, and the disputes among the intellectuals were of no consequence to him or her. There was a mixed populous: many who were conservative and nondoctrinal; a few who were seeking the truth and expecting to find it through a reform of the old ways. Cranmer and his Prayer Book offered much to both camps.

As A. G. Dickens said, that the Prayer Book was in English was probably the greatest shock. Once one got over that, the rest seemed normal enough. The Prayer Book retained the basic format of the various services. Whether or not the English was a precise translation of the original Latin was beyond the comprehension, and thus the concern, of most parishioners. If it looked the same—the same priest wearing the same vestments and standing, sitting, kneeling, and genuflecting at the usual times and places—the ordinary parishioner was not troubled. For the minority who took the words seriously, the effect perhaps could be troubling, for the wording, not the ritual, contained the ambiguities. The crucial wording of the Eucharist or Mass or communion service set the tone for the whole and determined the reception it would have in the wider society.

The Mass and the argument between Catholics and Protestants and between one group of Protestants and another over just what did or did not take place in this sacrament was both the root cause and the ultimate symbol of the chasm that separated one Christian from another. The Catholic doctrine of transubstantiation said that the bread and the wine were converted into the flesh and blood of Jesus at the prayer of consecration. This was in human terms a miracle. The priest who said the words was a worker of miracles. The flesh and blood of Jesus were being offered up once again as a sacrifice for the salvation of sinful mankind. The Mass was not the acting out of a once and previous Last Supper; it was the sacrifice of Jesus once again.

Every time Mass was said, Jesus died again. The bread and wine were in truth the very flesh and blood of the Christ in both his human and divine natures. This age-old doctrine was at the heart of what Protestants came to despise about the Catholic church. It comes as a shock to modern and more gentle ears to hear the words used by the reformers in attacking the Mass. "Superstition" was one of the gentler words used. One reformer wondered aloud about the progress of the bread and wine through the body of the recipient. If the recipient was receiving the body and blood of Jesus through the mouth, what was being excreted later from the rectum? Was it still the body and blood of Jesus? The crudity of the question should give a clear understanding of the great depths of anger, and even hatred, that the Catholic doctrine had engendered in the hearts and minds of reformers. A compromise would not be easy; nor was a compromise consciously desired by these reformers.

The movement of Protestant thought away from the Catholic doctrine of transubstantiation was neither easy nor direct. Luther had developed a position that has often been called consubstantiation. This is not as easily explained as is the Catholic doctrine. Luther said that body and blood were present and that the bread and wine were imbued with them because Jesus was always present everywhere. But, this meant that no miracle was being performed by a miracle worker; the "real presence" of Jesus was maintained without the efficacious role of the priest. This definition put Luther in opposition to Ulrich Zwingli, the Swiss reformer, who said that the communion was a service that commemorated the Last Supper. The divinity was present everywhere, but the human Jesus was not present in the bread and wine. Somewhere between these two extremes (transubstantiation and memorialism), Cranmer was to find his way. How he did so and the words used became the basis of Anglicanism.

Cranmer's second Prayer Book (1552) was very much a retention of the Sarum (Salisbury) Use in English. The modifications in the traditional Catholic canon were more in tune with traditional views of the early church fathers than with the recent views emanating from Wittenberg. The break with transubstantiation was not clear; the alternative to it was not clear either. What was clear is that the second Prayer Book clearly stated that Christ's sacrifice was a one-time event. Whatever else the Cranmerian communion might be, it was not a sacrifice of the body of Christ. The words Cranmer used were quite traditional: "this is my body; this is my blood." About the best one can say while trying to define just what Cranmer meant is the summation of Horton Davies in *Worship and Theology in England: From Cranmer to Hooker, 1535–1603:*

> through the Incarnation and Atonement there was a participation of the believer in Christ's flesh and that this was taught by the Sacrament but not effected by it.
>
> Cranmer's phase "spiritual eating" was no equivalent for figurative eating, but for the nourishment of the soul to a life beyond life, in short, a life with new dimensions of quality as well as of extension, eternal life. (P. 117.)

Saying that the body and blood were present for the person of faith was to adopt the Protestant position. The Prayer Books were seen as being part of a Cranmerian continuum, moving from Henrician Catholicism to a via media position. Those who looked only upon the 1549 book were not able to view the continuum effect. When Bishop Gardiner announced that he still saw transubstantiation in the 1549 Prayer Book, the reformers were convinced that he was right and they in turn were determined to reject it. The compromise had not worked, at least not in this first version of 1549. Cranmer himself was still evolving his own theology. The wider religious and political worlds were also moving into an era of greater confrontation.

Gardiner and others could also see many other signs of the old Catholicism in the Cranmer's first Prayer Book (1549). Prayers for the souls of the dead were retained, as was the veneration of saints and the Virgin Mary. The retention of auricular confession (if one's conscience agreed) and the use of anointing in baptism and Extreme Unction carried on all the symbols, if not the doctrines, of the seven sacraments. They in turn kept alive the symbols, if not the doctrines, of the old religion. Even though most, if not all by any means, of the content and format of the later Elizabethan Prayer Book (1559) were already in place in Cranmer's first book of 1549, the timing was unfortunate. As was already seen, Gardiner saw so much of the old in it that the reformers were moved to reject it. The conservative elements in the wider society were shocked by the English language, if nothing else. There was no one to defend the book. Somerset was inclined to toleration, or to mere indolence. The result was that the Prayer Book of 1549 and the first Act of Uniformity which enforced it were failures. The greatest loser of all, however, was not Cranmer or his book but Somerset himself. A serious economic crisis had been brewing and the issuance of the Prayer Book was both a cause of riot or rebellion in some places and the victim of rebellion in others.

REBELLION, NORTHUMBERLAND, AND A NEW PRAYER BOOK

A rebellion in Exeter and Cornwall in 1549 attacked the Prayer Book and expressed loyalty to the old religion. An even more serious rebellion in Norfolk in 1549 led by Robert Kett was largely based upon economic discontent, but it was also outspoken in its demands for greater religious reform. Somerset proved to be as tolerant, or indolent, in maintaining law and order as he was in maintaining religious uniformity. Both rebellions were crushed by local gentry and nobility. Somerset was crushed along with the rebels, being arrested and sent to the Tower by his opponents at court. The causes of the revolts were certainly economic; the precise issues are still uncertain. For generations, if not centuries, the causes were explained by reciting the one word "enclosures." Enclosures were the former common lands of the medieval manors that had once been farmed communally by the serfs and landlords. Ever since the labor shortages caused by the ravages of the Black Death in the fourteenth century, innovative landlords had expelled peasants from their ancestral holdings, fenced in the land, and converted to sheep farming. The expelled peasants either found work on other manors with labor shortages, went into the towns, or suffered the trials of beggary, vagabondage, or banditry. As Thomas More put it, "the sheep were eating the men." Starting in the sixteenth century, contemporaries and historians have always blamed economic difficulties upon the supposedly rapid expansion of enclosures. We now know that in fact there were fairly few enclosures in the sixteenth century. The great century for enclosure was the eigh-teenth, and even at the end of that century most of the manorial land of England was still not enclosed. But, whether enclosures were decisive or not, the rebels seemed to think so.

The economic grievances definitely took on a Protestant hue. The real causes of the economic distress were undoubtedly the debasement of the currency and the rapid increase in inflation. Both of these affected the middle classes and the workers in the towns, but even more they affected the farmers dependent upon cash crops. The very people affected economically were also those who were more likely to be interested in and have opinions about issues of wider import, such as religion. Recent research has shown that many of the participants in Kett's rebellion were landholders, not just agricultural laborers.

Somerset was the ultimate loser in the rebellions. He was blamed for allowing them to break out in the first place and was unable to get credit for their defeat. He was arrested by John Dudley, the earl of Warwick, and placed in the Tower. Dudley would soon become the duke of Northumberland and succeed Somerset in fact, if not in title. Where Somerset has had a repu-tation for being a good man and a tolerant ruler, both in church and state, Northumberland has always been seen as a nasty, greedy man who sought to impose a new tyranny upon the na-tion. More recent scholarship has not revised the view of nasty personality and character but has been more willing to see that he may deserve credit for restoring a greater efficiency to gov-ernmental administration, which was a welcome change after the decline in governmental effectiveness in the last years of Henry VIII and the "tolerant" administration of Somerset. After securing his own position, Northumberland released Somerset from the Tower and made some effort at cooperation. This did not work and Somerset was executed in early 1552, as their per-sonal and political needs were irreconcilable. At this point, Cranmer was ready with his revised Book of Common Prayer (1552), which was to provide the basis for an alliance among Northumberland, Cranmer, and the reforming, or Protestant ele-ments.

In 1550 Cranmer chaired a commission whose members were greatly influenced by followers of Martin Bucer and John a

Lasco. Bishop Gardiner's support of the first Prayer Book in 1549 had aroused fierce Protestant opposition to it. The commission issued the Ordinal (book of rules) of 1550, which specifically retained the historic ordained hierarchy of bishops, priests, and deacons. This was obviously a conservative act. The Ordinal of 1550's other main provision was just as obviously a radical one: the Mass was not to be seen as a propitiatory sacrifice performed by the priest. This was in keeping with the 1549 Prayer Book, which had already determined that Christ had died once and for all; he did not die again in the Mass. Even though the Ordinal was not all that new, the denial of the sacrifice of the Mass was a formal victory for the reforming party.

The revised Prayer Book that followed in 1552 was an even more clear-cut victory for the reforming party. It also represented the continuing evolution of Cranmer's own theology. While the new book retained much of the order of the first, it was clearly new, with a new, Protestant core. In the crucial rite of the Eucharist, the word "Mass" was dropped. The word "altar" was also dropped, being replaced by "communion table." The "altar" was also moved to the body of the church, running east and west in line with the nave. In name and in location, it was now clear that no sacrifice, indeed no miracle, was being performed. In the order of prayers, the "prayers of the people" were placed before the prayer of consecration, thus enhancing the role of the laity and of the community of believers while downplaying the role of the ordained clergyman. The downplaying of the clergy was enforced by the forbidding of most of the vestments traditionally worn by the "miracle-working" priests. The words said at the distribution of the bread continued to be "the body," but "take this in remembrance of me" was added. What did the new formula mean? Was it nothing more than a crude fudging of the meaning, or was there really a precise definition? Who knows? As has been suggested before, the confusion may be deliberate obfuscation. It may also mean that Cranmer had reached a solid theological position that this change truly represented, whether we understand it or not.

An indication of how conservative Cranmer was at the same time that he was leading a reform movement is seen in the controversy over the so-called Black Rubric. A rubric is a stage direction, such as "stand," "sit," "kneel," "genuflect," inserted in the Prayer Book before, during, and after the various prayers. The rubrics were printed in red ink, whence comes the name "rubric." The new Prayer Book retained the rubric calling for the communicants to kneel while receiving the bread and wine. This obviously carried traditional Catholic implications. The Privy Council ordered the insertion of a new rubric, printed in black in order to stand out from the red ones around it, into the final version of the Prayer Book. The Black Rubric, also called the John Knox Rubric, stated that kneeling constituted neither adoration of the elements nor an acceptance of the doctrine of the real presence. (John Knox was the militantly Calvinist preacher in Scotland.) The final version of the Prayer Book approved by Parliament in the Act of Uniformity of 1552 did not contain the Black Rubric since there was a more moderate leadership in Parliament. Whether the rubric was in or out, it was clear that Cranmer believed that the body of Christ was in Heaven, not in the bread and wine. Yet, he would still have people kneeling.

The commission continued to meet and issued a new document that more fully delineated the stand the reformers were taking on matters of discipline and organization. The document that they produced was named *Reformation Legum Ecclesiasticarum* by John Foxe, author of the later Book of Martyrs, which was to glorify those executed by Mary Tudor. The *Reformation* called for the continuation of excommunication and imprisonment for heretics and other violaters of the new rules. Divorce in case of adultery was allowed, as well as in cases of mistreatment and desertion. (None of these would have been proper grounds for Henry VIII to use against Catherine of Aragon.) Diocesan and provincial synods were to be established and would include representatives of the laity among the membership. A new class of lay elders or "seniors" was established to assist the priest in maintaining discipline. This system was similar to that used by Martin Bucer in Strasbourg and John a Lasco at his London Church of the Strangers. The first signs of presbyterianism (the use of representative governing bodies) were being seen. Whether because of this or for other reasons, Northumberland rejected the *Reformation*. Cranmer had been closely involved with the work of the commission, and had served on its inner steering committee. Did he, therefore, necessarily agree with everything in the *Reformation*? It was clear that Cranmer insisted that the validity of the *Reformation* depended upon its being decreed by the king, not by the commission. It was worded to imply that the young king himself was the author. On this point Cranmer continued to show a positive belief in a doctrine of royal supremacy. The rejection by Northumberland on behalf of the king was, therefore, conclusive as far as Cranmer was concerned.

Cranmer's work had its apogee in the second Book of Common Prayer in 1552. It had its conclusion in the formulation of what is generally called the Forty-two Articles. They, unlike the Prayer Book, were not to survive in such a pure form. The articles were the work of a commission and were revised by Cranmer. They contained several endorsements of previous writings, made several affirmations of faith, and also made several pointed condemnations. They were a mixed bag and would never have the simplicity that made for wide acceptance that the Thirty-nine Articles would later enjoy. The Forty-two Articles endorsed Cranmer's Book of Homilies, the Ordinal of 1550, and the second Prayer Book. They maintained that justification (salvation) was by faith alone, humans having no capacity for the performance of good works. They made a positive statement on predestination, but denied the existence of double predestination (believers in predestination were of two types: all believed that predestination meant only those specially chosen by God were going to Heaven; some also believed that it meant the rest were going to Hell.) The "positive" position was only concerned with Heaven. Hell and those destined for it were ignored. The Forty-two Articles also recognized the king as supreme head of the church. Further, the articles declared that all civil magistrates were lawful and were ordained by God; therefore they must be obeyed for conscience's sake, not just for human reasons.

Equally interesting were the various religious positions that the Forty-two Articles condemned. First were the Catholic items: transubstantiation, along with the idea of a sacrificial Mass. Christ was declared to be in Heaven; there was no real presence at the Eucharist. Purgatory was condemned, as was clerical celibacy and, of course, papal supremacy. The other attacks were largely aimed at the Continental Anabaptists. Their denial of Original Sin was especially to be condemned, and they also were accused of dispensing with the moral law. They had wrongfully allowed communal property, lay preaching, and the forswearing of oaths. Worst of all, they were accused of advocating universal salvation. The Anabaptists, of course, had taken reform way beyond what Luther and Calvin had ever attempted. The Forty-two Articles were a via media between Roman Catholicism and Anabaptism. So were Luther and Calvin. Where did that leave the Church of England? The Forty-two Articles left it very close to the position of the two great reformers.

Convocation approved the Forty-two Articles; Parliament did not even see them. By promulgating them, Northumberland was actually enhancing the royal prerogative. The king was indeed supreme head of the Church of England. Cranmer's work on the reform and structure of the church had been accomplished in cooperation with Convocation, but, even more, in close convergence with the views of the young king and the views and political needs of the duke of Northumberland. Cranmer's work (and soon his life as well) would end with the death of Edward VI.

Edward's health deteriorated and his approaching death forced Northumberland to move swiftly and unscrupulously to preserve his power and, indeed, to preserve his own life. The accession of Edward's Catholic sister, Mary, was to be stopped at all costs by the man who had so closely allied himself with the extreme (in the English sense) Protestant camp. He was hated for his religious stance and for being a greedy and grasping tyrant by a large section of the court and the country.

EDWARD'S DEATH AND MARY'S REIGN

Northumberland's scheme to save himself was really too clever by half, as it turned out. He claimed that young Edward VI had the right to determine the succession by will as Henry VIII had, ignoring the fact that Henry had been granted that right by act of Parliament. Without such an act of authorization, Northumberland advised the king to will the succession to the descendants of Henry VIII's younger sister, Mary, rather than to Henry

VIII's daughters, Mary and Elizabeth. Northumberland claimed that both were illegitimate, because of the annulments Henry had acquired in each case. Northumberland was, of course, also ignoring the fact that the daughters had subsequently been legitimized. By Northumberland's device, the crown must go to Henry VIII's grandniece, Lady Jane Grey, upon the death of Edward. Lady Jane had already been married to Lord Guildford Dudley, Northumberland's young son. Thus, upon Edward's death, Lady Jane would be queen, Lord Guildford would be king (consort), and Northumberland would be the father of the king, father-in-law of the queen, and chief minister in perpetuity. Clever, but it didn't work!

Lady Jane was proclaimed queen in 1553 and London secured. Mary (Henry VIII's daughter) was in Norfolk. Cranmer was among those who signed a letter asking her to accept Jane as queen and admit to her own illegitimacy. Mary's answer was to lead a rebellion and begin the march on London. Mary entered the city in triumph and was proclaimed queen. All the conspirators were arrested, including Cranmer, and all were sooner or later executed, including Cranmer (for heresy). What was the nature of the church and state over which Mary now ruled? What changes would she make? Why?

Whether Cranmer had consciously sought to create a via media or not, the very idea of a via media was totally foreign to Christians of the sixteenth century. In the traditional view, one was either a true (orthodox) Christian or a heretic. In the new post-Reformation view, one could be a Catholic, or a Lutheran, or a Calvinist, or whatever. Even a general Catholic-Protestant division was years away. The fact of the matter was that one was expected to fully adhere to whichever denomination was established. The wrong choice could be dangerous. The Church of England at the death of Edward VI was not Catholic. It is less clear as to what it was. If a neutral observer saw a via media, that was because he or she could not see anything else with clarity. In the long sweep of European Christianity, if a church was not Catholic, it was Protestant. By this form of reasoning, England was Protestant. One proof was that the Roman denial that Anglican bishops and priests were validly "ordered" stems from the Catholic decision that the Ordinal of 1550 represented a break with

the Catholic tradition. The Ordinal of 1550 had specifically retained the historic orders of bishops, priests, and deacons. Rome
never accepted the underlying explanations for their retention.
In Roman Catholic eyes, the Church of England was Protestant.
As Luther had repeatedly insisted, the Catholic church was a papal church or it was nothing. A church that was nonpapal was
therefore not Catholic. England was Protestant.

Mary was joyfully proclaimed and accepted as queen in 1553
not because she was Catholic, but because she was Henry's
daughter and the heir by lawful right. Lady Jane and Northumberland might have inspired a disputed succession and civil war.
Mary, however, represented legitimacy and stability, and she
was accepted for these reasons, not for herself or her religion.
Since the 1530s the church had been the province of the monarch. This was to be honored again. If Mary were Catholic, so be
it. Because the Edwardian Church was established by law, the
restoration of the Catholic religion would require the use of law.
Laws that could be enforced in the courts of common law and
laws that could lead to the death penalty had to be enacted by a
parliament. Mary summoned a parliament soon after her accession. How far the two houses cooperated with her not only determined the success of her program but also revealed the real
priorities of the lords spiritual and temporal and the common-
ers in Parliament. The assumption made by many modern historians that the dissolution of the monasteries and the wholesale
disposal of the lands had created a class of wealthy men who
were wedded to Protestantism has no basis in fact. As was made
clear by the Marian parliaments, the retention of their newly acquired lands was the only part of the Henrician settlement that
was sacrosanct; parliament wouldn't touch it.

Mary was a gentle, kind, and sympathetic woman. In other
times and in other circumstances, she may well have been a figure upon whom history could look kindly. Such was not her fate;
"Bloody Mary" she soon became and "Bloody Mary" she was to
remain for most Englishmen. Among her other traits was a total
dedication to the Roman Catholic church, the total restoration
of which became the all-consuming goal of her existence. The
perpetuation of the restored Rome in turn depended upon her
having a legitimate heir. She was determined upon marriage,

and marriage to a Spaniard, at that. This would mark the complete repudiation of her father and all his actions against her, her mother, the pope, and God. The emperor Charles V decided that the Spanish match would be with his own son and heir, Philip, duke of Burgundy. A parliamentary outcry was countered by Mary's decision to marry Philip—he was both a foreigner and a Catholic. The declaration of marriage was in October 1553, upon the opening of her first parliament, and the marriage took place the following July. Loyalty to Spain was now combined with loyalty to the pope. The mixture was disastrous for Mary and for the Catholic cause in England ever since.

The new parliament moved very slowly in carrying out Mary's program. The acts of Edward's reign which had established the Protestant faith were repealed, but this left the church where it had been at the death of Henry VIII in 1547. Mary was, like it or not, "Supreme Head on Earth of the Church of England." Like it, she did not, since she could not head the Church of England and remain Catholic. The Henrician church was not fully restored in that the expanded heresy laws required positive reaffirmation; they were not reaffirmed. The queen removed Cranmer from his post as archbishop of Canterbury, leaving it vacant for two years. Her principal advisers were to be Stephen Gardiner, the former bishop of Winchester, who was both restored to that see and appointed lord chancellor, and Reginald Pole, who was to become a cardinal and papal legate, and finally archbishop of Canterbury. Pole especially provided the link between Mary and Rome. Gardiner was a somewhat more typical minister of an English crown.

The new year began with the most dangerous threat from rebellion faced by any English government in the Tudor era. Sir Thomas Wyatt and his men from Kent entered London and constituted a force of three thousand men within musket shot of the court. Whereas the Marian government had become completely identified in the public mind as a combination of Catholicism and Spain, and Wyatt represented the equally clear Protestant and English alternative, the stress in both cases should be put on the national designation, "Spain" vs. "England," as being the more important. The pro-Spanish Marian court defeated the rebels and began the first of the long series of executions that marked Mary's reign. Lady Jane Grey and her young husband, Lord Guildford, were executed. Princess Elizabeth, seen as a threat, was sent to the Tower and began her long struggle of survival, at which she became such a master. Parliament showed its continuing resistance to Mary by refusing once again to reenact the Henrician heresy laws and the Six Articles. Resistance from Parliament did not prevent the court from pursuing its goals. All married clergy were expelled from their livings, with many going into exile on the Continent. The total expelled was about two thousand, or a quarter of all the priests. The impact on London was particularly acute.

In all the pushing and shoving back and forth in 1553 and 1554, the opposition to the Spanish match was greater than the opposition to Catholicism. There was in fact some evidence that the Catholic Mass was again being said voluntarily in parishes throughout the kingdom. Also, there was evidence that the lay orders of brotherhood, or guilds, that were common in the generations preceding the Reformation and were eliminated by the dissolution of chantries in Edward's reign were reappearing. Their comeback indicated the need by the laity to participate in the church as a community of believers. Many lay persons found less opportunity to participate in the new Protestantism than in the old Catholic fraternities. The Protestant movement was still very much directed by the leadership; change came from the top down, tradition came from the bottom up.

ROME RESTORED

From spring until fall of 1554, Cardinal Pole and Queen Mary kept up the pressure on Parliament to complete the Catholic restoration. That the restoration needed parliamentary authorization was theologically anathema to the Roman church, which was going through its own reevaluation in conjunction with the Council of Trent, which was reaffirming traditional Catholicism. All attempts to move Rome in the direction of conciliating Protestants had been rejected in its early sessions. Protestantism was heresy and was to be extirpated. The true faith came from God through the Catholic church, and the English Parliament should follow the teachings of the Catholic church, not presume to determine what those truths were. Like it or not, however, Mary, Pole, and the pope had no choice: they must either submit to the indignity of pleading for parliamentary authorization or forgo the restoration of the Catholic religion. There could be no restoration of Catholicism except by act of Parliament. The deal was struck, and in November of 1554 Parliament restored the heresy laws and treason laws and repealed all antipapal legislation enacted since the fall of Wolsey in 1529. The one exception was the dissolution of the monasteries and the chantries, which had meant the abolition of the regular orders of monks and nuns. England was once again a Roman Catholic nation, although still without monasteries and nunneries.

Mary and the Roman church did not have long to enjoy their triumph. The court was convinced that the land reeked with heresy; Mary agreed. By June of 1555 the trials of supposed heretics began their relentless course. The victims included a few famous names, such as Hooper, Ridley, Latimer, and the archbishop of Canterbury himself, Thomas Cranmer. Whereas the somewhat comparable trials in the reign of Henry VIII had resulted in the deaths of a few famous men, such as More and Fisher, the Marian trials went way beyond the mere setting of a few conspicuous examples. About three hundred in all were convicted and executed before it all came to an end with Mary's own death. The public reaction slowly mounted, and Spain and the Roman church shared the opprobrium with Mary in the long run. In the short run, however, Philip decided to preserve his own position and returned to Spain to sit upon his newly acquired throne.

John Foxe, an Oxford University fellow and ardent Protestant, fled to Germany at the first hint of a Catholic restoration. While there he paid close attention to events in England and began the preparation of a book that was to become nearly as influential as the King James Bible and the Book of Common Prayer—*Acts and Monuments of These Latter and Perilous Days,* or Foxe's Book of Martyrs, as it is commonly called. Foxe, not Mary, really had the last word.

Thomas Cranmer has often been compared with Thomas More, to the former's disadvantage. More has been praised for being willing to die for his conscience. Cranmer has been ridiculed for vacillating and only reluctantly accepting death at the end. The two cases are not exactly comparable, however. More was both certain and consistent in his refusal to accept Parliament's right to use its legislative powers to undo fifteen hundred years of European history. The issues that Cranmer faced were more complex. He had been a confirmed believer in the royal supremacy almost from the beginning of his religious pilgrimage; he had also become a committed Protestant. During the reigns of Henry VIII and Edward VI his two principles were in union; during Mary's reign they were in direct conflict. Which of his principles should take precedence—royal supremacy or Protestantism? Because Mary had used the royal supremacy to repudiate itself and to restore the pope, logic (if nothing else) called for Cranmer to decide in favor of Protestantism, which in the end he did. While tied to the stake he extended the hand that had earlier signed his recantation into the flames. This was hardly the action of a weak or cowardly man. Rather, Cranmer's conduct during this crisis was symptomatic of the crisis that the nation itself was going through. The belief that the people and the monarch should share the same religion was deeply ingrained throughout Western Europe. It was Mary and her advisers who forced Cranmer and England itself to choose. Once Mary combined mass burnings at the stake with a pro-Spanish foreign policy, all in the name of the Roman church, the eventual triumph of a monarchical English Protestantism appeared to be inevitable.

THE DEATH OF MARY

Philip's departure, of course, ruled out any last hope that Mary would bear an heir. Philip, however, had not forsaken England altogether. He persuaded Mary to join him in a war against France, which he fought solely for Spanish interests. The pope, Paul IV, supported France in order to protect papal interests in Italy. When Philip refused to stop the war, Paul excommunicated him. While under the pope's ban, Philip persuaded Mary to declare war on France. Just as earlier Cranmer had to choose between the royal supremacy and Protestantism, Mary now had to choose between the pope and her husband, the king of Spain.

She chose Philip and war. The war required forced loans for its financing, Parliament being in no mood to levy the needed taxes. The loans exacerbated the already strong anti-Spanish (soon to be anti-Catholic) feelings in England. The loss of the war and of Calais, the last English possession on the continent of Europe, were devastating to Mary. She believed that her last hope for earthly redemption lay in the birth of an heir. She became convinced, with no shred of justification, that she was pregnant, even going into "confinement." Her death in 1558 spared her and England even greater sorrows. Her legacy was the English conviction that Roman Catholicism meant tyranny in domestic policy and treason in foreign policy!

Princess Elizabeth and her chief adviser, Sir William Cecil, had managed to stay alive and to retain the hope of Protestantism in the wider nation. They both joined the English people in heaving a sigh of relief at Mary's passing. If Mary had not died, there might well have been another rebellion, with incalcuable consequences. Elizabeth and Cecil had honed their considerable natural political skills during Mary's mercifully short reign. They were joined in their hour of triumph by the rapid return to England of the hundreds of laymen and clergy who had fled to the Continent as exiles—"the Marian Exiles."

4 / THE ELIZABETHAN
SETTLEMENT

ELIZABETH THE QUEEN

The reign of Elizabeth I (1558–1603) and the Elizabethan religious Settlement marked a watershed in English history. She and the Settlement are quintessentially English—the via media or the Aristotelian Golden Mean. The great irony is that no one has been able to state with any assurance just what Elizabeth herself believed in, if anything. Perhaps her lack of obvious religious commitment made it possible for her to adopt, enforce, and perpetuate the Settlement. Perhaps a clue to her underlying position can be seen in her words and acts during the first days of her reign. She quickly issued a declaration calling for the continued enforcement of the existing religious laws, Marian and Catholic. She also forbade unlicensed preaching, which was a deliberate attempt to deny the returning Marian Exiles a ready pulpit. It was thus clear from the start that the law of the land, whatever it said, was to be dominant in religious as in all other matters. Under Elizabeth, obedience to the laws was more important than the true faith (assuming that there was one). That the reign would be Protestant, not Catholic, was implied, however, in the form that the royal title took. The Henrician and Edwardian title had concluded with the words "Supreme Head on Earth of the Church of England." Mary, not wanting such a title, had substituted "etc." for this whole phrase, implying that she was not supreme head. Once Mary had had the offending clause repealed with the restoration of papal supremacy, a law-abiding Elizabeth could not on her own restore the clause. The temporary solution was the addition of the "etc." to the Marian title, implying that she might well be supreme head. So the law was the law, but the hint of a Protestant restoration was there. A further hint was seen when the queen received the wine along with the bread at communion, and allowed English in the liturgy and the Lord's Prayer. The Catholics retained some hope for their future; the Protestants were anxious for the full realization of their dreams. There were to be many disappointments for both groups.

The new queen was to have no honeymoon period. The Marian Exiles were flocking back eager for office and/or livings and a dominant voice in the new dispensation. A more moderate group under the leadership of Richard Cox returned from Frankfurt. A more militant group that had gone to Geneva with John Knox were a greater problem. Knox himself had already issued his *A First Blast of the Trumpet against the Monstrous Regiment of Women* and was not allowed into England because of his extreme religious and political views.

Many of the Exiles received high clerical or ministerial office, including Cox, who became bishop of Ely. Of the twenty-six bishoprics, ten were vacant because of deaths. One Marian bishop took the prescribed oath to Queen Elizabeth, but the other fifteen Catholic bishops refused and were removed. Thus twenty-five new bishops were needed. Until the new appointees replaced the Catholic incumbents, the House of Lords still had a strong Catholic bias (some of the lay peers had been ennobled by Mary). Their strong legacy of Catholicism meant that Convocation would be largely ignored by the court in the fashioning of the new dispensation. The House of Lords would also be a problem for Elizabeth. This left the House of Commons as the central forum, and it had what could probably be called a Puritan majority, with "Puritan" meaning members of the Church of England who wished to make the new church as clearly Protestant as possible. They were not seeking a via media.

SUPREME GOVERNOR OF THE CHURCH

When the first parliament of the reign met in January 1559, the sixteen Catholic bishops were still in the House of Lords and the concurrent session of Convocation affirmed its loyalty to the Catholic position. The Protestants' position was less focused than the Catholics'. The latter were willing to accept the return of the royal supremacy; the former were divided among those who wanted a return to the full Henrician church, the Edwardian church of the 1549 Prayer Book, the Edwardian church of the 1552 Prayer Book, or some less clearly defined Genevan model. The two things all sides could still agree upon were the retention of episcopacy or bishops; and the royal supremacy. Debates raged around whether or not communion should be in both kinds—bread and wine. The Protestants argued over the administration of the sacrament more than they did its meaning and substance, although no one could be unaware that the deeper meanings were at bottom what they were arguing about. Although Elizabeth took no direct role in the debates, she showed her hand by receiving communion in both kinds. At last the two houses of Parliament and the queen were able to agree upon a package that included the Act of Supremacy and the Act of Uniformity. It is not absolutely clear what finally brought the arguing to a head and enabled the passage of the acts. One widely held view is that once the Treaty of Cateau-Cambresis was agreed to among England, France, and Spain, the queen could declare her Protestantism more clearly and reach a conclusion. The treaty called for French and Spanish acceptance of the Elizabethan crown of England. It also ended, temporarily, the enmity between France and Spain that made it necessary for Elizabeth to offer some hope to the Catholic religious position. England was safer when France and Spain were enemies and it could play one off against the other. Ever since the break from Rome, England had feared a French or Spanish (or both) attack upon England. Religion and foreign policy were always linked.

The Act of Supremacy was in the end a compromise with the Catholic position. Elizabeth was supreme governor but not supreme head of the Church of England. "Supreme head" was generally defined as being the highest rung on the clerical ladder, virtually an English pope; "supreme governor" was defined as being over the clergy but not one of the clergy. Catholic as well as Protestant clerics opposed the idea of a female cleric, but there was another issue as well. The Henrician royal supremacy had implied, if not declared, that the king had sacramental as well as administrative powers, whereas the "governorship" implied no such thing; it made Elizabeth nothing more than chief magistrate. These were not arguments over mere words, nor were they arguments over the possibility of a female member of the clergy. To deny the *potestas ordinis* (priestly power) to Elizabeth, and to all of her successors as well, was to make the royal supremacy a little bit less exalted. If the monarch were no more than the holder of the *potestas jurisdictionis* (administrative power), then Parliament might have an excellent claim to some share in the governing of the church. If the English monarch were a true pope, then Parliament had little claim to a share in that power. If the church was merely a branch of government then parliament could claim a voice. Neither Elizabeth nor her successors prior to the Glorious Revolution liked to admit that Parliament had a share in the religious jurisdiction, but no Parliament ever renounced its own claims. The Act of Supremacy was to be one of the continuing issues that divided king and Parliament, church and state, court and country.

THE ACT OF UNIFORMITY

The Act of Uniformity that followed the Act of Supremacy, both of 1559, called for compulsory attendance at church on Sundays and holy days and specifically reinstated the Book of Common Prayer of 1552 (Cranmer's) with some modifications. The 1552 Prayer Book had been a large step in the Protestant direction; the Elizabethan modifications were largely in a conservative (Catholic) direction. Kneeling at the communion was retained, but the Black Rubric, which had stated that kneeling implied no adoration of the elements, was repealed. The queen herself seems to have taken the lead in making these "conservative" modifications. The Elizabethan Settlement, therefore, was greatly influenced by Elizabeth herself. The Book of Common Prayer of 1559 would be revised slightly in 1604 and again in 1662. It continues to be the liturgy of the Church of England to this day. (The 1980s saw the adoption of an Alternative Services Book for trial use, but it does not yet have official status. The 1662 Prayer Book is still used in the presence of the queen.)

The standardization of the liturgy was not, however, to put an end to all disputes. The Prayer Book itself was largely silent on ornaments and vestments; their continued usage became highly contentious issues, encapsulated within the word *adiaphora,* or "unessentials." Over the centuries the Catholic church had developed a vast wardrobe of vestments and a great panoply of ornaments, from candlesticks to wine cups or chalices. The use of any or all of these items had become completely associated with the Roman church itself. All the reformers, including Erasmus, had to confront the issue of ornaments and vestments. Because few if any of the specific objects were mentioned in the Bible (the New Testament in particular) their retention in a reformed (Protestant) church reminded the true reformer of the old Roman church and could make him or her question the fullness and the sincerity of the reform. Who but a real Roman Catholic would want to look like a Roman Catholic? The retention of Roman objects indicated that the old religion was still alive. There also were theological differences which overlay fundamental institutional differences between the Catholic and the reformed or Protestant systems. To dress as a Catholic priest, to perform the communion service at an altar decorated in the Catholic style, and to go through Catholic-like motions was to be a Catholic as far as the true reformer was concerned. The true reformed faith, therefore, required the full elimination of all offending objects and practices. The true biblical religion should be conducted in a pure biblical fashion. The convinced reformers became known as "Puritans" or "precisionists." They were still in the church but would spend most of a century trying to "purify" the Church of England of all relics of what ought to be a dead past. For the true church of the Bible to be clearly seen by all, the old ways of a corrupt and corrupting priesthood should be expunged forever.

The seeds of future conflict were sown in the very wording of the Elizabethan communion service. The 1549 Prayer Book referred to the bread as "the body of our lord Jesus Christ" and the 1552 Prayer Book said "take and eat this in remembrance of me." The Elizabethan Prayer Book of 1559 incorporated both phrasings, thus taking a position that could well be considered Catholic by anyone who wanted to. The Ornaments Rubric of 1559 specifically authorized the use of the altar at the communion and also called for the wearing of the alb, chasuble, stole, and cope, which had been called for in the 1549 Prayer Book. The 1559 Prayer Book also added some confusion by using the word "minister" in the services of morning and evening prayer, but "priest" for the communion service. This clever compromise as seen by modern historians was a dangerous confusion for Elizabeth's contemporaries. Most true reformers thought and expected that the 1559 Prayer Book was just a stopgap, ending the Marian Catholic era, but not yet providing the true reformed church that most of the Marian Exiles dreamed of. But, as has been said above, if the basic definition of a Roman Catholic is the recognition of papal supremacy, then the England of Elizabeth was indeed Protestant. The queen herself for the rest of her life would take credit for having rescued the realm from the clutches of Rome. She really spoke of herself as the new Moses who had led her people out of the new Egypt (Rome). The preservation of the new order would take constant and determined efforts on her part. A few of her clergy shared her concern for the new church. The new archbishop of Canterbury, Matthew Parker, was one of them.

Parker had been chaplain to Anne Boleyn and his ties to her daughter were strong indeed. He had spent the Marian years in England, not in continental exile. He had married in the Edwardian reign, but had put his wife aside during Mary's reign. He, like Cranmer, would probably have preferred the life of a Cambridge don to that of the premier prince of the church. He does not seem to have taken a lead in defining the new settlement, unlike his predecessor. His role was largely one of giving full support to the queen once decisions were taken elsewhere. Parker and Bishop John Jewel, the author of the Apology of the Church of England issued in 1562, would undoubtedly have been associated with the views expressed at the end of the reign by the "Judicious" Hooker (as we shall see later) if they had been alive at the time. They both represented what was later seen as the Anglican via media.

Besides the support of such men as Parker and Jewel, the queen had support, albeit in a Protestant direction, from Sir William Cecil, her secretary of state, who kept an eye on the Privy Council. Elizabeth also had the ability to strike swiftly when necessary. The situation in Scotland presented a great opportunity. John Knox, barred from England but not Scotland, had arranged for the expulsion of the French forces supporting Mary, the Franco-Scottish Catholic queen of Scots, and took power for the Protestant cause through the Lords of the Congregation, a self-appointed group of Protestant landlords. The Treaty of Edinburgh that followed left Mary with her title, opportunities for mischief, and the frustrations of being lectured to by John Knox. The treaty also guaranteed that the British island (which included Scotland) would be Protestant. There no longer was a Catholic base on England's border. Mary would herself quickly destroy her remaining welcome in Scotland and become a "guest" of her English cousin. This will be treated in greater detail below.

THE THIRTY-NINE ARTICLES

The Act of Supremacy and the Act of Uniformity had been enacted by Parliament in 1559. The third base of the new church, the Thirty-nine Articles of Religion, was to be the work of Convocation, not Parliament. The queen preferred to have as much as possible concerning religion out of the grasp of Parliament. This enhanced her role as supreme governor of the church, as she was seen doing important things without Parliament. The Thirty-nine Articles of 1563 are still the foundation of the worldwide Anglican communion, whether or not any clerical and lay members today even know what they are. They quite clearly represent the clergy's own commitment to the reformed or Calvinist faith. By her commitment to them the queen cemented the bond between her and the church and between herself and the Protestant reformed faith. She remained loyal to the articles, even if no one else did. Because they are so much a part of the Anglican tradition and because all candidates for ordination in England must still swear acceptance of them, they are listed and commented on here.

1. Belief in the Trinity—Father, Son, and Holy Ghost (Spirit).
2. The Son has two natures, 100 percent human and 100 percent divine; He was born of the Virgin Mary.
3. Following His death, Jesus descended into Hell.
4. Jesus rose from death "with flesh, bones, and all things appertaining to the perfection of Man's nature."

5. The Holy Ghost proceeded from the Father and the Son and is of one substance with them.

6. The Bible contains all things necessary for salvation; nothing can be required that is not in the Bible (the books of the Old and New Testaments are each named).

7. The Old Testament is fully compatible with the New; although rules governing ceremonies and rites no longer apply, all the moral commandments are fully binding.

8. The three historic creeds are accepted: Apostles', Nicene, and Athanasian.

9. All descendents of Adam are born of a sinful nature (Original Sin) and are thus inclined toward evil or the "desires of the flesh." Those baptized are no longer to be condemned for the Original Sin.

10. Since the fall of Adam, humans do not have free will or the ability to work their own salvation; the grace of God makes good works possible.

11. Jesus died to save us and through the faith alone can we be saved.

12. Good works flow from the faith and are, therefore, pleasing to God.

13. Works done before receiving the grace of God are not pleasing to God; in fact, they may be sinful.

14. Works of "supererogation," or those works that go beyond what God commanded, constitute arrogance and impiety.

15. Christ was fully human except that He had no sin; baptism washes away sins, but our human nature still makes us prone to further sins.

16. Because humans can and do sin after baptism, there is room for repentance and forgiveness for these sins.

17. "Predestination to Life is the everlasting purpose of God . . . and our Election in Christ, is full of sweet, pleasant, and unspeakable comfort to Godly persons . . . ."

18. Only in the name of Jesus Christ can any human being find salvation.

19. The visible church of Christ is a congregation of faithful people in which the word of God is preached; the churches of Jerusalem, Alexandria, Antioch, and Rome have all erred in their ceremonies and beliefs.

20. The church has the power to decree rites and ceremonies and to determine controversies over matters of doctrine, as

long as nothing contrary to Scripture is done and no part of Scripture can be used against another part of Scripture.

21. General councils of the church are called by secular leaders; attended by human beings, they are subject to error; therefore, they do not have authority over the Scriptures.

22. Purgatory, pardons, images, relics, and the invocation of saints are all without scriptural foundation and are repugnant to God.

23. No one is allowed to preach before the congregation without having been properly called by those with the authority to do so.

24. No "tongue" is acceptable in church that is not understood by the congregation.

25. Sacraments are ordained by Christ and are badges or tokens of Christian beliefs and signs of grace and God's good will and they "strengthen and confirm our Faith; Christ ordained two sacraments, baptism and the "Supper of the Lord." The other so-called sacraments—Confirmation, Penance, Orders, Matrimony, and Extreme Unction—are not found in the Gospels and are not, therefore, on the same level as the first two. Sacraments are not "to be gazed upon, or to be carried about"; those who misuse them will be damned.

26. The efficacy of a sacrament does not depend upon the nature or quality of life of the minister, although the church should enforce proper discipline and aim for a worthy body of ministers.

27. Baptism separates the Christian from the non-Christian and is a sign of a new birth; the baptism of the young is to be retained as being compatible with Christ's ordinance.

28. The Lord's Supper is a "Sacrament of our Redemption by Christ's death: insomuch that to such as rightly, worthily, and with faith, receive the same, the Bread which we break is a partaking of the Body of Christ; and likewise the Cup of Blessing is a partaking of the Blood of Christ." "The Body of Christ is given, taken, and eaten, in the Supper, only after an heavenly and spiritual manner. And the means whereby the Body of Christ is received and eaten in the Supper is Faith." Transubstantiation is "repugnant to the plain words of Scripture."

29. "The Wicked, and such as be void of a lively faith, although they do carnally and visibly press with their teeth (as Saint

Augustine saith) the Sacrament of the Body and Blood of Christ, yet in no way are they partakers of Christ; but rather, to their condemnation, do eat and drink the sign or Sacrament of so great a thing."

30. The people should receive the "Cup of the Lord" along with the bread.

31. Christ died once and for all for all mankind; He does not repeat His sacrifice over and over again whenever the Mass is said.

32. Members of the clergy are allowed to marry or not as they please.

33. Those cut off or excommunicated from the church can be reconciled through penance and restored to the community of the faithful.

34. All persons should honor and respect those traditions of the church that have been established by competent authority. "Every particular or national Church hath authority to ordain, change, and abolish, ceremonies or rites of the Church ordained only by man's authority, so that all things be done to edifying."

35. The Book of Homilies appended to these articles as well as the homilies from the reign of Edward VI are to be used in churches.

36. The ceremonies for consecrating bishops and ordaining priests and deacons as prescribed in the Prayer Book of 1549 and retained in the Act of Uniformity are the proper rites by which a valid clergy is ordered.

37. The monarch is the chief governor of the realm over all estates, civil or ecclesiastical, but the monarch does not have the powers of the clergy (*potestas ordinis*). "The Bishop of Rome hath no jurisdiction in this Realm of England." Capital punishment may be established by law for "heinous and grievous offenses."

38. "The Riches and Goods of Christians are not common, as touching the right, title, and possession of the same, as certain Anabaptists do falsely boast"; but Christians should give generously to the poor, according to their ability.

39. Vain and rash swearing is forbidden, but Christians may "swear when the Magistrate requireth, in a cause of faith and charity, so it be done according to the Prophet's teaching, in justice, judgment and truth."

Article 29, about the condemnation of the "wicked" who take communion, was dropped by the queen at the initial approval of the articles and was restored in 1571. It represented a strong Calvinist view. Therefore, the Thirty-nine Articles were actually the Thirty-eight Articles for a period of eight years. With this one alteration, the body remained intact. The whole weight of the articles is on the side of a via media. There were explicit denials of Catholic doctrines and practices, but there were equally explicit affirmations of doctrines contrary to the "best reformed opinion." The whole closely resembles the Forty-two Articles that had been issued with Cranmer's close participation. The Elizabethan Prayer Book was largely that of 1552, with some items returning to the 1549 version. The whole Elizabethan Settlement can be called a via media, and Thomas Cranmer can clearly be seen as its chief author. If Cranmer had not been cut down in his prime by Catholic Mary, who knows how much further his own views might have evolved? What Cranmer had accomplished by the death of Edward VI was to become his own and England's permanent legacy.

DEBATE WITHIN THE CHURCH

As has been pointed out above, except for Cranmer (and even in his case it may well have been unconscious), no one sought a via media for its own sake. The Elizabethan Settlement as it stood in 1563 was taken by no one, except perhaps by the queen herself, as being carved in stone. The Catholics may have had to accept a certain Protestant inevitability, but the reform-minded (soon to be called Puritans) still thought that the whole religious system was to be fought for. The discontented would attempt to use the various church institutions, such as Convocation. When they found that the church would not reform itself, then they turned to Parliament. The Puritan movement was, therefore, a struggle for the nation's soul both within the church and between the church and the state. The queen was at the center of the whole affair, whichever arena was chosen for the contest. The supreme governorship was to prove to be the central and decisive fact about the Church of England. It was the supreme governorship that made it the Church of England.

The points that would be most in contention during Elizabeth's reign were less centered upon particular articles as they were upon omissions from the articles or the actual implementation of the Elizabethan Settlement. For some, the retention of Catholic ornamentation and vestments merely gave the wrong image; for others, the retention of the episcopacy became a bone of contention. This was especially the case as bishops proved themselves to be unwilling or unable to effect changes. If they could not do the work of the Puritans, then they were expendable. Others rejected the whole structure of the church, including the royal governorship; they would eventually become the various bodies of separatists. Most of the critics did accept the royal governorship and the establishment of a state church. Most Englishmen were Erastian, in that they favored a state-dominated church, even if they had little else in common. Where the royal governor found advisers and sharers of the royal power would increasingly be an issue. Was the queen expected to share her authority only with the bishops, with the bishops and the wider body of clergy represented in Convocation, or with the nation represented in Parliament? It was this third contention that created so much of the stuff of politics for more than another century.

THE VIA MEDIA

As was pointed out in the preface, the heart of religion is not just doctrine. Doctrines reflect and represent ways of life and thought about life and its meaning. It is necessary, therefore, to look more closely at the Anglican via media and its impact upon the lives of the people within its fold. What of the old had really been retained? Would that which was new be satisfying? Was the middle way a new way, or was it really just the old way in new garb?

The nature of the Elizabethan church (the via media) can be summed up by saying that the outward signs, the clerical hierarchy and the Prayer Book liturgy, were Catholic, whereas the inward part, the doctrine, was Protestant. The mix could not have been the other way around—Protestant governance and liturgy combined with Catholic doctrine. The reason is not only that one could not have the Mass without the priest. A more important reason is that the majority of the English people were conservative, traditional, and illiterate. An ordinary Englishman expecting the traditional comforts from religion could attend the Elizabethan church and see a familiar clergyman, dressed in familiar garb, going through the familiar motions, but saying in English words that had never been understood in Latin anyway. For an educated, sophisticated man from London or the university towns, the wording of the prayers and of the Thirty-nine Articles was sufficiently open to a Protestant interpretation that he could accept it as being up to date or at least headed in that direction. The via media was, therefore, a mix that aimed different messages at different segments of the population. It should not, however, be assumed that mix was only a clever political ploy; it was the only way such a mix could have been constructed and it flowed naturally from the point on the religious continuum from Catholic to Protestant reached by Cranmer, Parker, Elizabeth I, and those who had to enact it into law. One of the reasons why the Elizabethan Settlement lasted is that the timing was perfect.

The great stress that historians have put upon the role of the Puritans and their successors since the middle of the nineteenth century, and the lesser but increasing interest that some historians have taken in the surviving Catholic tradition, have tended to distort the picture of the religious life of the average Englishman of the sixteenth and seventeenth centuries. The modern student can too easily assume that everyone was either a Puritan or a Catholic, united in opposition to a royal establishment forcing a religious conformity that was alien to the mass of people. A much more accurate view is that the mass of English people accepted the Elizabethan Settlement and the Prayer Books and have been Church of England (C of E) one way or the other since its inception.

Certainly the old Catholic religion was no longer the religion of the mass of people. As J. J. Scarisbrick has written, "... the theology...of belief in Purgatory, the sacrificial efficacy of the mass, veneration of saints was the very antithesis of Protestantism.... The new creed denied the priestly (i. e., sacrifical) role of the cleric, much of his sacramental function and his 'apartness'. . . . '"[1] On the other hand, there is no evidence that the mass of people were dedicated to the Biblical and predestinarian earnestness that is associated with the name of Puritan. Patrick Collinson[2] suggested looking at the summary of the nature of English religiosity given by Richard Kilby in 1618 in his *Halleluiah, Praise ye the Lord for the unburthening of a loaden conscience.* Kilby said of "popular religion": ". . . the multitude doubtless conformed in great numbers to the prayer-book religion of the parish church, which became part of the fabric of their lives. . . . Is not this your religion? I meane, to say your praiers, to heare service etc., without any spetiall stirring of your heart? And was not such a religion all one with that which you call the old religion [C of E]?"

A fundamental change had indeed been brought about by the fact that the church was now established by law and buttressed by an Act of Uniformity and an Act of Supremacy. The frequency of participation in church was no longer just a matter of personal conscience and community pressure; weekly attendance was now required by law and failure to attend could result in a fine. Furthermore failure to attend could be looked upon as both a religious and a political statement. The ultimate loyalty was no longer to a pope in Rome but to a queen in England.

Another fundamental change was the actual interior of the church building. The reformed tradition opposed the use of images out of fear of idolatry and superstition. As a result, statues were removed from churches, murals were painted over, and stone- and woodwork was removed or destroyed. The Puritan tradition, if not the whole Protestant transition, was iconoclastic. In place of images of the Virgin Mary and the other saints was a model of the royal coat of arms. In song and poem, the Virgin Mary was increasingly replaced by the Virgin Queen. The rood screen, behind which the Catholic priest had celebrated Mass, was removed, and the parishioners could now view the

---

1 J. J. Scarisbrick, *The Reformation of the English People* (Oxford: Basil Blackwell, 1984), p. 39.
2 Patrick Collinson, *The Religion of Protestants: The Church in English Society, 1559–1625* (Oxford: Clarendon Press, 1982), p. 191.

clergyman directly. The installation of pews was another great change; pews meant parishioners no longer wandered around the church socializing or doing business during Mass. They remained seated and listened to the service (now in English, not Latin) and to the newly important sermons, into which the Puritan clergy in particular were putting much effort. However, there is no proof that the mass of people felt as spiritually uplifted by these changes as Puritan writers and their dedicated followers wanted to make everyone believe.

The Reformation resulted in a succession of administrative and financial changes in the church as well. Some of these changes affected the lives of ordinary people directly, others only indirectly. One of the things that helped Henry VIII get the support of most of the episcopal hierarchy during the years of the break from Rome was that much of the money previously sent to Rome would now stay in England and in the episcopacy's hands. The same was true of ecclesiastical court cases in that cases that had traditionally gone to Rome now remained in England. The traditional levies on the people continued: the tithe was still collected, along with the hearth tax, which had come to be called Peter's Pence. The traditional levies on the clergy were also retained: annates were still paid by a newly appointed bishop. The difference made by the break from Rome was that these monies were retained by the highest level in England, which previously would have received them only before passing them on to Rome. In the case of the bishops, what they received from those below stayed with them. Their own payment of annates to the pope stopped. In the case of court appeals, the court of the archbishop was now the highest court, appeals to Rome being cut off. The episcopal beneficiaries of the break with Rome did not, of course, object to it. What they may not have anticipated was the speed with which Henry VIII and Thomas Cromwell created royal substitutes for the papal coffers. Later monarchs would also toy with the establishment of royal courts in place of the old papal courts.

Cromwell saw to the institution of a Court of Augmentations, which received monies from the dissolved monasteries, and a Court of First Fruits, which effected the diversion of annates from the pope to the king. Once these courts were in place, the people and the clergy were paying as much as before, but to the king, not the pope. Court appeals that had gone to Rome and had rested temporarily with the archbishops were also transferred to the king via his Privy Council. In fact, the judicial committee of the Privy Council still has jurisdiction over the clergy in religious matters. A very important statute at the beginning of Elizabeth's reign had a very great impact upon the church itself and its relationship to the crown. The so-called Exchange Act of 1559 allowed the crown to effect an exchange with the diocese of a newly appointed bishop so that royal rights to certain revenues from landed properties would be granted to the bishop in return for comparable ecclesiastical manorial rights accruing to the king. The exchange benefited the crown because royal estates were generally managed much less efficiently than ecclesiastical estates. The result of this act was the rapid impoverishment of the episcopacy. The enrichment of the crown was more difficult to document, because its financial state throughout the sixteenth and seventeenth centuries was always precarious at best.

The financial plundering of the church began with the modest reform of a few monasteries during the leadership of Cardinal Wolsey and took a quantum leap forward when Henry VIII and Thomas Cromwell dissolved the monasteries. The work continued with the abolition of the chantries in the reign of Edward VI. All of this, however, had been at the expense of the monastic orders and the saying of masses for the dead. The Reformation, from a purely theological point of view, had no place for either of these institutions. The Elizabethan Exchange Act, however, was an attack upon the secular clergy and the bishops in particular. This resulted in a great deal of confusion over the role and place of bishops in the new order of things. Both the queen and the Puritan critics of her church had their reasons for challenging the bishops. The queen, however, would have very important reasons to support the bishops as their existence helped the queen govern the church. Although bishops would remain an essential part of the Church of England, their place in society would be greatly modified by their decline in economic status. This episcopal decline would also be mirrored by changes on the parish level, which saw a significant increase in the standing of the parish priest.

The parish priest's increased standing in society in the face of economic decline was itself a mark of the true religious revival that accompanied the Reformation. The break from Rome may have been a political act and the push may have come from on high, but one result was an increased interest in religion in general throughout society and in the written Bible or prayer book. The increased interest in the written word led to an increased demand for a "learned clergy." This became a point of controversy. The crown seemed to be reluctant to encourage a more learned clergy, on the assumption that a learned man might be more likely to think for himself. A man learned in the Scriptures might also be learned in the writings of continental reformers and be more likely to question, if not challenge, the admittedly loosely defined religious establishment.

The economic decline of the clergy during Elizabeth's reign meant that the bishops were like princes in their power and authority but more like the gentry in their incomes. They were dependent upon the crown for any alleviation of their financial plights. Bishops were allowed to marry and have children, but their less-than-princely incomes made it difficult to provide for their families. The lower clergy had an economic status below that of yeomen, although their social status was akin to that of the gentry. An increasingly learned priesthood could tend toward breakdowns in discipline if the crown were not careful. Preferential treatment at court could be one solution to economic hardship. A strong following among a prosperous and enlightened laity could also provide economic opportunities. The Elizabethan church had a great deal of potential trouble within its ranks. The economic position of the clergy, combined with theological differences, provided a frame for turmoil. The lack of clearly defined positions on many points of theology was a blessing in that it dampened enthusiasm but was also a source of continued conflict for those who chose to fight.

THE ROMAN CATHOLICS

The place of the remaining Roman Catholics in Elizabethan England requires some attention. About 10 percent of the English people remained loyal to the old religion. Mary's reign was clearly their last chance at the center of power. Catholics and Protestants were thoroughly disgusted with the burnings of heretics and the military losses in a Spanish-led war. Most of the Marian bishops were forced to vacate their sees after the passage of the Act of Supremacy. Most of the parish clergy also left office, although some did take the necessary oaths of allegiance and retained their positions. Within the nation, Catholicism remained strongest in the north and among the northern aristocracy and gentry. To what extent lay Catholics sought peace and quiet in their own faith, or sought instead to join fellow Catholics in overturning the heretical Elizabethan church, varied. Throughout the reign, Queen Elizabeth assumed that the great majority of Catholics were in fact loyal to her and to England. Their response at the time of the conflict with the Spanish Armada in 1588 was to prove her right. The outside forces— including the papacy, the Spanish crown, the supporters of Mary, Queen of Scots, and the large number of Catholic English clergy who were trained on the Continent—were to create grave problems for the queen directly and indirectly by generating a virulent anti-Catholicism among her Protestant subjects in and out of Parliament.

During the first decade of Elizabeth's reign, the Catholic powers on the Continent hoped that she would become Catholic or would marry a Catholic and secure a Catholic succession to the throne. In the absence of a child of her own, Mary, Queen of Scots, was her heir. The future for the Catholic cause did not seem hopeless by any means. Philip of Spain offered his own hand in marriage and was politely refused. Offers from the Catholic dukes of Anjou and Alencon also were forthcoming on a regular basis for years on end. The most enthusiastic Protestant members of Parliament, however, were adamant in their dislike of a Catholic marriage. They were also adamant in their dislike of the probable succession of Mary, Queen of Scots. The only solution for them was a Protestant marriage for Elizabeth. One of the many sources of conflict between the queen and her parliament was over the question of their right to advise her as to marriage. In her eyes, such an obviously personal matter was by definition solely a royal prerogative. The queen's failure to marry a Catholic, or anyone else, and Mary Stuart's virtual imprisonment, led to total frustration in Rome and the determination to take action in England. The duke of Norfolk, the successor to the man who had put down the Pilgrimage of Grace in the reign of Henry VIII, offered to marry Mary, Queen of Scots. This was tantamount to a declaration of war as far as Elizabeth and Sir William Cecil were concerned.

THE NORTHERN REBELLION
1569

Ever since the break from Rome, the dissolution of the monasteries, and the Pilgrimage of Grace, the north of England and its nearly feudal aristocracy increasingly resented the centralized rule from London, which was in the hands of such relative upstarts as Sir William Cecil. The more conservative north had come to despise the rule of men such as Thomas Wolsey, Thomas Cromwell, and now Sir William Cecil, all of whom sought to strengthen the rule of the center at the expense of the provinces. The latter two were Protestant, and therefore the objections were religious as well as political as far as the north was concerned. To the political, economic, and religious discontent was added concern over the succession to the throne, the dynastic ambitions of the Howards, and the machinations of the Florentine banker Roberto di Ridolphi.

The first phase of the crisis was the Northern, or Earls', Rebellion, which was decisively crushed and put an end to noble rebellions. To that extent, the Middle Ages were finally at an end; there were to be no more such noble rebellions. The crown would in future years have the support of the nobility. Ridolphi and Norfolk continued their plotting and, in fact, plotting on behalf of Mary Stuart continued one way or another for the next eighteen years, ending only with the execution of Mary herself. Ridolphi was convinced that there were many Catholic Englishmen who would welcome the overthrow of Elizabeth and the accession to the throne of the Catholic Mary, Queen of Scots. He plotted with both Mary and the Catholic duke of Norfolk to effect the removal of Elizabeth. The plot was more the work of Ridolphi than of Norfolk, although his marriage to Mary was part of the scheme. The key element was to be a Spanish invasion which would secure the success of the English rebellion and place Mary and Norfolk on the English throne.

THE RISE OF ANTI-CATHOLICISM

In the midst of the Northern/Ridolphi crisis, Pope Pius V took precipitate action and in 1570 issued the papal bull *Regnans in Excelsis*, which excommunicated Elizabeth, deposed her, and called for her overthrow. The bull was illegally drawn, in that it did not give the queen the requisite year in which to conform before sentence was pronounced. From this time forward, Catholics in England would be forced to carry the additional burden of treason (for Catholicism was now considered tantamount to treason) on top of the already heavy burdens of tyranny and love of Spain that were the fruits of Mary Tudor's reign. To talk and act in a tolerant fashion was to be very difficult, if not dangerous, for Elizabeth until the defeat of the Spanish Armada in 1588.

The founding of a Catholic college at Douai in France in 1568 by William Allen and the entry into England of two Jesuits, Edmund Campion and Robert Parsons, in 1580 added to the religious strife and demand for action. Jesuits were considered to be the special agents of the pope, committed to the overthrow of Elizabeth. There was little the queen could do to hold back the surging tide of anti-Catholicism. In 1581 the laws requiring Catholics to attend the Church of England were strengthened. The new laws were called the Recusancy Laws. The fine for nonattendance was increased from one shilling per Sunday to twenty pounds—a truly exorbitant sum for any but the wealthiest. To convert to Roman Catholicism was treason punishable by death. To be a Jesuit was treason punishable by death. By the end of Elizabeth's reign, about 250 Catholics had been executed.

THE DUTCH REVOLT

Anti-Catholicism on the one hand and pressure from the Puritans for reform of the Church and the removal of Mary, Queen of Scots, on the other were both part of a wider problem that Elizabeth had to face. The first two-thirds of her reign was dominated by a series of crises that were all linked in one way or another to the Dutch Revolt. Elizabeth's handling of the Dutch Revolt and all its consequences has become a classic example of political realism and crisis management for students of international relations ever since.

The Dutch Revolt for independence from Spain became an open conflict in 1566. Even though the population of the Netherlands was divided between Protestant and Catholic, and the leading rebel, William the Silent, himself was a Catholic, the revolt was perceived throughout Europe as being a fight between Dutch Protestants and Spanish Catholics, since this was in fact the simplest way to see it. In a world increasingly polarized by religion, it seemed only natural to the bulk of English people that Protestant England should sympathize with, if not actively support, the presumably Protestant Dutch. Spain, which had become so thoroughly disliked during the reign of Mary Tudor, became the successor to the French as England's natural enemy. The Dutch Revolt was to be the focal point for Elizabeth's reign, involving her marriage, the succession to her throne, her relationship with the Puritan factions within the Church of England, and her relationship with an increasingly outspoken opposition within Parliament. In the eyes of the mass of her subjects, a good Protestant queen would marry a Protestant Englishman; would secure a Protestant succession thereby; and would take all necessary steps against Mary of Scotland (killing her was preferable; removing her from the line of succession was the minimum acceptable). The ultimate proof of her loyalty to the Protestant cause would be her support of the Dutch. From the point of view of an increasingly unhappy group of reformers in the church and in Parliament, the queen's position (or lack thereof) on the church and on the Dutch issue was highly confusing and fraught with great danger for the Protestant cause and for England itself.

The reign of Bloody Mary and the bull *Regnans in Excelsis* had created a fear and hatred of Catholicism that exceeded the expressed fears of Elizabeth herself. Many felt the queen was not taking sufficient interest in the dangers to her throne, to the true Protestant faith, and to England. For them, the ultimate enemies were the pope and the Roman Catholic church that he led. Protestant England viewed the Catholic church as being inspired by

Satan himself, and the pope as the true anti-Christ. It was God's will that these evil forces be expunged from England, if not from Europe as a whole. Because the Roman church was the embodiment of evil, why would anyone want to look or act like a Catholic? If Rome has ordained clergy who wear vestments, as well as services with altars, beeswax candles, pipe organs, and the like, all true Christian churches should remove such "evil" remnants of a Catholic past. The retention of so many Catholic forms and practices in the Elizabethan church could lead Protestant zealots to question the faith and the patriotism of Anglicans, including the queen herself.

THE RISE OF PURITANISM

This national fear and abhorrence of the Roman church and pope played directly into the hands of the Puritan reformers. They had not succeeded in purging the Elizabethan church of Roman vestments; the conflict, known as the Vestiarian Controversy, peaked in 1567 and 1568. The failure to achieve this highly visible and deeply symbolic reform led quickly to the rise of presbyterian sentiments. If a church governed by bishops would not reform, perhaps what was needed was a church without bishops. This was something no queen or king would willingly contemplate. The Genevan model for presbyterianism was one where the local congregation chose its pastor as well as delegates to higher-level synods or assemblies. The flow of authority was from the local parish or congregation upward. This was just the opposite of the Church of England and Anglican structures, where authority flowed from the top down. No monarch or pope would ever accept the presbyterian alternative; Elizabeth and the pope had at least this in common. (What James I meant by "no bishop, no king" was clearly understood by Elizabeth I.)

Because the bishops themselves were in place and were under the ultimate authority of the queen, steps to effect a change in structure had to begin elsewhere. The House of Commons soon became the base of operations for the new presbyterian Puritans. Such reformers as Thomas Cartwright, Walter Travers, and Peter Wentworth made great names for themselves over the next few years. Cartwright and Travers were scholars,

Wentworth was a member of Parliament. By resorting to the House of Commons to effect reform, they escalated the controversy into a great constitutional as well as religious conflict. The queen could no more tolerate an expanded role for Parliament in ecclesiastical affairs than she could tolerate the replacement of bishops by presbyters.

The seeds of conflict between the crown and Parliament over their respective roles in the church had been sown by Henry VIII when he carefully enshrined every step in the break with Rome in parliamentary legislation. Even though all the bills were worded in such a way as to deny innovation and to affirm what had always been the law, the fact is that great numbers of parliamentarians over the ensuing years thought that Parliament was "legislating" new things into being, such as the Act of Supremacy of 1534. The crown's position on the role of Parliament was very clear. The church was under the crown! The Parliament's role was to create laws providing for the punishment of those who broke the laws, including church laws. God had made Henry the supreme head; Parliament made it a crime to deny it. It is not surprising, however, that those who were not too sophisticated in legal niceties thought that Parliament had made him supreme head by passing the Supremacy Act.

Henry VIII had refined an arrangement between the House of Commons and the king at the time that Thomas More had become Speaker of the House of Commons in 1523. The basic issue had been the definition of "free speech." The definition agreed to, which was still operative as far as Elizabeth I was concerned, prohibited Parliament from acting on or even discussing those matters that came within the royal prerogative without the crown's consent. On those matters that were properly before the House of Commons, members could vote for or against bills and explain why they favored or opposed them. They could not, however, impugn the motives of the crown's ministers who had introduced bills that might be opposed. To speak in a way that could be construed as encouraging opposition would be fraught with difficulties.

This definition of "free speech" was directly attacked in 1571 when Walter Strickland, "a grave and ancient man of great zeal," introduced a bill to revise the Book of Common Prayer. Such a bill was a direct attack upon the royal prerogative. The bill got nowhere and was followed in 1572 by Cartwright's *Admonition to Parliament*, which attacked the existence of bishops within a "reformed" church. John Whitgift, the master of Trinity College, Cambridge, published in 1572 his *Answer in Defense of Bishops*. Cartwright responded with a second *Admonition* in 1572, which resulted in his being expelled from England by the crown in 1573 for attacking the bishops. In the midst of all this there occurred the Massacre of St. Bartholomew's Day in Paris on August 24, 1572, in which 25,000 or more French Huguenots (a Protestant group) were killed at the instigation of Catholic leaders by a Parisian mob. Although the English Puritans had nothing of this kind to fear, the massacre further convinced them of the evils of Roman Catholicism. The failures of the *Admonition* debate and the Prayer Book reform in Parliament were followed by a new controversy—over "prophesyings."

"Propehesyings" were public sermons expounding the teachings from the Gospels that were delivered less in a learned manner than in the manner of one who was directly inspired by God. Anyone not already in agreement with such a preacher was usually repelled by the sermons. Certainly, the queen was moved to have them cease forthwith. The first Elizabethan archbishop of Canterbury, Matthew Parker, had died in 1575. His successor was Edmund Grindal, a staunch Puritan, whose first assignment was to prohibit prophesyings. He refused to do so and was suspended within a year of taking office. He was not a man who could be co-opted. Upon Grindal's death in 1583, the queen appointed as archbishop John Whitgift, the defender of episcopacy and the royal governorship. By this time, some determined reformers began to despair of the Church of England altogether and seceded from it. This was not at all acceptable, either politically or constitutionally.

These first "separatists" were followers of Robert Browne, whose views about the need for each individual to express his or her own experience of the divine made any organized cooperation with others who did not share those views almost impossible. Even the presbyterian structure required working with groups other than one's immediate neighbors. Implicit in separatism was congregationalism, the autonomy of each parish.

This in turn meant secession from the national body politic. The English nation was divided into shires or counties within which were urban chartered communities known as boroughs. Within the shires and boroughs the next level of government was the parish. The parish had a rector or vicar, elected lay wardens, and a clerk. The lay officials had what now are considered governmental responsibilities. Secession was akin to what South Carolina did in 1861, and Elizabeth regarded it in about the same way that Lincoln did. Submission to the crown or exile were the only real alternatives in the sixteenth and most of the seventeenth centuries.

There was another major issue on which the queen and her religious supporters differed from the growing Puritan faction, and on this issue the queen would have more in common with Catholics than with Protestants. That issue was the place of the individual human being in the wider social structure. The classical and medieval Christian concept of the "great chain of being" recognized a hierarchical universe with the purely spiritual God at the top and the purely material earth at bottom. From the inanimate earth the hierarchy progressed upward from plants to animals to humankind—a soul (spirit) within a body (matter). Beyond humans were the angels—more spirit than matter—and then God—all spirit. This universal chain of being had its companion in the organic theory of society. If all human life is in an organized society (as Aristotle insisted), then the queen was the head or brain and everyone else played a greater or lesser role in relationship to the head. These various parts each performed a different and specific function within the well-ordered whole. A happy human is one in whom each part plays its assigned role and each part is given the concern or treatment that its assigned place warrants. A foot is not a brain; a wise brain, however, does not mistreat the foot. The organic view of life was completely compatible with the Roman Catholic and medieval traditions of hierarchy in both church and state. The Puritans had largely accepted a Calvinistic (more than Lutheran) view of society and the individual. Calvinists stressed the sovereignty of God and the depravity of natural human beings. (The Lutherans were more accepting of traditional society, headed by a king or nobleman.) The only distinction between one human and another was the issue of predestination. Some were of the elect; most were damned.

For the Roman Catholic, the word "vocation" meant the call by God to special service, generally as a member of a clerical order. The English Protestants in Elizabeth's reign began to use the word in a purely secular manner—the practice of a skilled profession or trade. The secularization of "vocation" signified a basic split between the Catholic and Protestant views of life and of the world. Members of the clergy in Catholic doctrine were a special kind of human being who had a role to play in transmitting the saving grace of Christ. For the Protestants, clergymen were ordinary humans with special training and skills. Some people were lawyers, some were tailors, some were butchers, some were ministers of the Word. The humanizing and professionalizing of the clergy had an impact upon the wider society. Once the gap between clergy and laity was eliminated, one learned or skilled person was as a good as another. Any learned person endowed with the faith could read and interpret the scriptures as well as the next person. The result was a stress upon Scripture, not the liturgy or the clergy, and upon the efficacy of each individual to determine his or her place in society and in relationship to the Divine.

THE APPROACHING CRISIS

As the years went by and the queen was getting beyond child-bearing age, and therefore beyond marrying age as well, the potential for crisis increased. Because she did not have an heir, the line of succession to the throne still led to Mary, Queen of Scots. This, of course, was totally unacceptable to her Protestant subjects in general and to the Puritan faction in particular. The great advantage was that Spain was not likely to invade England or work too hard at overthrowing Elizabeth if the principal beneficiary would be Mary and her French connections. As long as Mary lived, however, domestic Catholic plots to overthrow Elizabeth came one after the other. This was a dangerous atmosphere for anyone to live through. However, Mary also kept Spain at bay. On balance, the price of keeping Mary alive was worth paying, unless the domestic threat became too great. Elizabeth's tolerance of Mary's existence also encouraged the Puritan elements in Parliament, at court, and in the country to portray themselves as being better Protestants, and perhaps better patriots, than the queen herself. This attitude of the Puritans merely reinforced the queen's disgust for and distrust of them and made them seem to be a greater threat to her authority than the English Catholics. The queen was also buffeted by the Puritans for her lukewarm response to the Dutch rebels' call for help.

The deaths of the duke of Alencon, Elizabeth's principal suitor, and of William of Orange in 1584 quickly transformed a dormant hostility between England and Spain into a bitter cold war and then into the almost-inevitable hot war. The fact was that Elizabeth would not get married and that the Dutch needed help. The state of war with Spain would wax and wane until Elizabeth's death in 1603, when peace was made. To shore up the Dutch after William of Orange's death, she dispatched English troops under the command of her particular friend, the earl of Leicester. Offered the Dutch crown, she refused it and all the obligations to the Dutch cause that it entailed, such as England paying to liberate Holland. Leicester infuriated her by accepting the post of governor in Holland; his acceptance implied a greater commitment on the queen's part than she was willing to make. Leicester's activities on the field of battle were as inept as his grasp of politics and diplomacy. Philip II naturally was annoyed by Leicester's actions, and his patience with England and Elizabeth was reaching its limits.

Patience at the court of Mary Stuart was also reaching its limit. Over the years there had been many attempts to liberate her and/or to overthrow Elizabeth on Mary's behalf. Mary herself was party to some of these plots. The deaths of Alencon and William of Orange and the dispatch of troops to Holland were accompanied by a most serious plot against Elizabeth—the Throckmorton Plot. It was discovered and stopped, but was soon followed by Babington's Plot. This was also discovered and resulted in Mary's arrest, trial, and conviction. These Catholic plots against Elizabeth were on behalf of Mary. Whether she was personally involved is still not known to this day. Her sentence was death by decapitation. On the first of February, 1587, Elizabeth signed the death warrant. She also gave instructions that it was not in fact to be executed without her further authorization. But executed it was on February 7, 1587. Mary's death evoked rage from Elizabeth, real or feigned. Her secretary, Davison, who had ordered the execution, was imprisoned and fined, and Burghley and Leicester were banished from court. Soon, however, all were restored by Elizabeth in fact if not in name. Elizabeth was free from plots at home, but now that Mary and her French connection were gone, Philip II had no reason to delay his descent on England, because he alone would be the beneficiary of a successful invasion.

The story of the Spanish Armada has been told many times, and never better than by Garrett Mattingly in *The Armada*.[3] Whether the English triumph was due to God and the "Protestant wind" that He caused to blow, or to the tactics and seamanship of the English, or to the poor strategy, tactics, and luck of the Spaniards, is the stuff of which many books and legends are made. Suffice it to say that the Spanish "enterprise of England" failed and England was spared invasion, possible conquest, and possible civil war.

AFTER THE ARMADA

The defeat of the Spanish Armada was the beginning, but not the end, of a long war with Spain. Domestically, it was a watershed in England's religious life. The English Catholics had proven to be loyal, as the queen had always assumed they would be. Their willingness to fight the Spaniards when the crunch came satisfied most Protestants that the queen and England were securely Protestant. The only religious problem for the remainder of Elizabeth's life and reign came in the months right after the defeat of the Armada. The Marprelate Controversy and the series of tracts issued from 1587–89 in the name of Martin Marprelate (the "hammerer of the clergy") were a great but short-lived renewal of the earlier Puritan attacks upon the episcopacy and the supreme governorship. The latter made the movement especially dangerous, and a careful search ensued for the author or authors and the printer or printers. The author was never found, but in 1589

---

3 Garrett Mattingly, *The Armada* (Boston: Houghton Mifflin, 1959).

the printer was found and imprisoned. The controversy might be seen as the last gasp of Elizabethan Puritanism. Although Puritan ideals certainly lived on in many hearts and minds, no one was to foment a crisis either in Parliament or at court during the remainder of Elizabeth's reign. The Irish Rebellion and the earl of Essex's attempt to seize power in London would provide the "crisis" with which the reign ended. What the Marprelate Tracts did generate, however, was a controversy within the hierarchy of the established church about the true nature of episcopacy and the true meaning of the royal supremacy. The fruit of this debate was Richard Hooker's *The Laws of Ecclesiastical Polity.*

Bishop Richard Bancroft had attacked Marprelate by taking the position that the origins of episcopacy were biblical. Bancroft had been joined by Archbishop Whitgift in stating that the office of the bishop was both apostolic and divine in origin and had existed since the time of Christ himself. The divine nature of the episcopacy could be a potential denial of the royal supremacy, although the queen herself does not seem to have been concerned. In the midst of this dispute over the origins and nature of episcopacy the "judicious" Hooker produced what was soon to become the classic statement of the Anglican position on the nature and structure of the church and of its relationship to the crown and the wider society in general.

Richard Hooker had been a protégé of Bishop John Jewel of Salisbury and Archbishop Whitgift. *The Laws of Ecclesiastical Polity* drew upon their ideas and through them back to Stephen Gardiner and the Henrician view of the relationship between church and state as seen through the role played by the monarch. Hooker clearly stated what has become known as the "one-kingdom theory," as opposed to the "two-kingdom theory." The former declared the unity of church and state: "There is not any man of the Church of England but the same man is also a member of the commonwealth; nor any man a member of the commonwealth, which is not also of the Church of England."[4] It was clear that Hooker believed that church and state are one, and under the king or queen. But he defined this more fully when he

4 Richard Hooker, *The Laws of Ecclesiastical Polity,* book 8 (London: Church and Paget, 1888), p. 2.

wrote that "things indifferent" to salvation (*adiaphora*) were subject to parliamentary authority: "We are told it a thing most consonant with equity and reason, that no ecclesiastical law be made in a Christian commonwealth, without consent as well of the laity as the clergy, but least of all without consent of the highest power."[5] The role of the queen was primary, but the reference to laity and clergy meant Parliament. The queen did not challenge Hooker's book, but she certainly did not intend to share her royal authority with the House of Commons. Hooker agreed with Elizabeth that the "two-kingdom theory," or the separate but equal status of church and state, was not for England.

The "one-kingdom theory" tended to inextricably link birth and baptism. Hooker took baptism seriously, and infant baptism of English children meant that at birth one became both a subject of the crown and a "child of Christ." The two thus became synonymous. The only possible rival to the authority of the monarch within Hooker's system was Parliament. As outlined by Hooker, the struggles of the future would not be between church and state but between monarch and Parliament. If "church" and "state" are one and the same, then the question is, who has the power over the "church-state," the king or the parliament? The last decade of Elizabeth's life and reign saw even that struggle put "on hold."

---

5 Ibid.

5 / THE EARLY STUARTS AND THE RISE OF PURITANISM

A NEW KING

As Elizabeth I was dying, Robert Cecil sent his messenger north to Scotland to inform James VI of his imminent succession to the throne of England. James was more than ready to accept his divine appointment. The son of Mary, Queen of Scots, made a royal progress to London, receiving the happy acclaim of the English people, who had been subject to a half-century of female rule. James the man, not James the Scotsman, was warmly received. His journey south through England was marked by many events that showed his lack of knowledge about England and his assumptions that he had more to teach the English than they had to teach him. For example, he had a captured thief hanged without a proper trial. The Scotland that he left behind, although it was becoming increasingly Anglicized, was still thoroughly foreign. It was a small country with its own legal traditions, and since the accession of the infant James VI, it had been a country with its own religious and political systems. The state was much more loosely structured than in England. As king of Scotland James was poor, both in revenues and in power over church and state. The theoretical retention of an episcopal structure within the church fooled no one, least of all James. Scotland was presbyterian; power flowed from the bottom up. James had already stated in his *True Law of Free Monarchy* his fully developed intellectual concept of "divine right" monarchy. He also was convinced that he was destined by birth to be such a king. Scotland was too small a world for such as he. It was to be in England that he could be the "free" monarch that God and nature had intended him to be.

While on his progress to London James was handed the famous Millenary Petition (a thousand names, but none known to
us) demanding religious reforms. Even though James was de-
lighted to have shaken the dust of presbyterian Scotland from
his shoes, the English Puritans naively operated under two mis-
apprehensions: that a new monarch would mean a new religious
order, and that James must be a presbyterian, or at least a "cov-
enented" or committed Protestant. The signers were to be
proven wrong on both counts. James was concerned with pre-
serving what he thought to be a proper royalist religious settlement already in place in England, and he was no presbyterian.
The petition was the work of Elizabethan Puritan moderates, not
radicals. James's response was then and is still a puzzling one.
Instead of rejecting the petition out of hand and attempting to
track down its authors, he called a special church conference to
meet at Hampton Court Palace in 1604. The adulation that the
clergy bestowed upon the newly arrived king made him feel as
though he truly were the "British Solomon" who should quickly
seize the opportunity to demonstrate his wisdom before the
grandest in the realm. He not only called the conference, he also
presided over it.

THE HAMPTON COURT CONFERENCE

James's personal religious views were both traditional and tolerant. He was primarily concerned, not with theology, but with his
own royal power. As long as his power was secure and unchal-
lenged, he did not have rigid views that he sought to impose
upon others. He was not anti-Catholic, but he was antipope. He
was was not for or against particular points of Protestant doctrine or ritual as long as the law was obeyed and the royal supremacy was secure. He did not in *The True Law of Free
Monarchy* claim to have the *potestas ordinis* (clerical power),
merely the *potestas jurisdictionis* (administrative power). He
was no Henry VIII. He was willing to listen to the moderate Puritans and did not make their lives unbearable within the church.
The separatists, such as the Pilgrims, migrated in his reign, but
not the Puritans. It was James's son Charles I who troubled the
Puritans.

In 1599 James wrote his *Basilikon Doron,* an address to his son and heir, Prince Henry. In it he called the Scottish Puritans, who were like English separatists, "very pests in the Church and Common-weal." They were threats to the jurisdiction of the civil magistracy. Andrew Melville, the John Knox of his generation, called the royal views "Anglo-pisco-papistical." James went before the assembled clerics at Hampton Court quite clear in his own mind as to how far he would go; that he agreed to meet with the opposition at all was a real departure from the custom of his royal predecessors. The proclamation calling the meeting clearly stated his position: "Our purpose and resolution ever was, and now is to preserve the estate as well Ecclesiastical as Politic, in such form as we have found it established by the Laws here, reforming only the abuses which we shall apparently find proved."

The first session was open only to the bishops, deans, and privy councillors. James seems to have thoroughly enjoyed showing off his erudition in things biblical and his ability to reason out the solution to apparent inconsistencies. The bishops were literally bowing and scraping before him. Although he admitted that there were corruptions that needed reform, he essentially supported the church as he found it. Archbishop Whitgift fell on his knees, thanking God for giving England a king who was "so wise, learned and judicious."

The following day the Puritans were admitted and given a chance to speak. James showed more tolerance for their feelings, if not their views, than did the bishops. Richard Bancroft, the bishop of London, became so carried away in his opposition that the king stopped him and almost apologized to the Puritans for his behavior. Most of the topics brought up on both days were those taken from the Millenary Petition and concerned what James considered to be *adiaphora,* or things inconsequential: could baptism be performed by a woman, could it be performed in private, could it be performed by a layman? These issues dominated the first day and part of the second. What angered Bancroft was the Puritan view of predestination, which he said was aimed at overthrowing the church, not reforming it. Even though the Church of England, through the Thirty-nine Articles, officially accepted the doctrine of predestination, it was

already becoming more completely identified with presbyterianism than with Anglicanism. If one were predestined for
salvation, the sacramental liturgy would be unnecessary. Conse-
quently, one could jump to the conclusion that talk of predestination was really talk about the abolition of bishops. This
"logical" next step led to one of the more famous encounters at
the conference.

John Reynolds, master of Corpus Christi College at Oxford
University and essentially a moderate Puritan, had been the
leading spokesman for the Puritan cause. James had come to his
aid when the subject was baptism and a learned clergy. However, James saw in Reynolds a clone of Andrew Melville, the
Scotsman, who was close to Cartwright and Travers and openly
lectured James, when the subject of church governance arose.
Reynolds probably sought nothing more than some restrictions
on bishops' powers, but when he said the word "presbyterian,"
James fell into a rage, accusing the Puritans of wanting to abolish episcopacy. "Then Tom and Dick shall meet and at their pleasure censure me and my Council and all our proceedings...I
know what would become of my supremacy. No bishop, no
King." This famous phrase succinctly stated the issue then and
for the next generation.

James presided over the final session of the conference and
summarized its work in his own words, even granting a special
dispensation from the prescribed ceremonies for parishes in
Lancashire, thus showing a spirit of toleration. Although the
summary of the proceedings seemed to imply concern for and
concessions to the Puritans, the overall result of the conference
was a hardening of the established system and a rebuff of its
critics. When asked for a further extension of the Lancashire
dispensation, James said "Let them conform themselves and
that shortly or they shall hear of it." In the words of James's
biographer, D. H. Willson, "Conformity was to be one rigidly
enforced; and the Church was headed not towards greater comprehension but towards a hard and narrow exclusiveness. In this
fateful decision the King's will was a vital factor."[1]

---

1 D. H. Willson, *King James VI and I* (London: Oxford University Press, 1956), p.
209.

James's conduct of the conference turned what began as a moderate desire for reform into an opposition party that ultimately would seek the overthrow of the church (and the monarchy itself). By wrongfully accusing the reformers of wanting to abolish episcopacy (and monarchy), James had totally misjudged them and the situation. If to seek reform meant being a presbyterian, then so be it. Many were willing to make the leap. Thus James fathered a presbyterian opposition rather than burying it. The Church of England was in danger of becoming a mere denomination among others, although the only denomination established by law. The crucial question was: what does the name "Church of England" mean? Did it mean the church of all the English people, comprehensive in structure, doctrine, and ritual? Or did it mean a narrowly conceived structure with a precise core of doctrines and a uniformly enforced system of rituals that outlawed any and all opposition within or without its ranks? James and his bishops, deans, and privy councillors had chosen the latter. Their successors after the Restoration of 1660 would do the same.

The Hampton Court Conference may have had greater negative effects than positive in the long run. However, one great decision of incalcuable importance was made. James announced that a new Bible would be commissioned. Fifty-four translators headed by Overall, Reynolds, and Chadderton, took the earlier Bishops' Bible of 1572, which had been used in church in place of the Puritans' *Geneva* Bible, and produced, with the Authorized Version of 1611, one of the great monuments to the Christian religion and to the English language. It was to quickly join the Book of Common Prayer and Foxe's Book of Martyrs as one of the foundations upon which the English language, the English church, the English home and family, and public discourse would be built. The "King James" Bible was, until the late twentieth century, the basis for most other English translations of the Bible, including those of other Protestant denominations and Reform Judaism.

THE PARLIAMENT OF 1604

Early in 1604 James met Parliament for the first time. The most significant act of this first parliament was the adoption of the

Form of Apology and Satisfaction, which was a restatement of the moderate Puritan position on church reform, albeit recognizing the king's role as supreme governor. Parliament also declared that writs of heresy would be issued by the king, not the bishops, authorized clerical marriage, and ended alienation of episcopal lands. The Form of Apology said that the king could not interfere in debates in the House of Commons. The moderate reforms in the church were to be effected by acts of the king-in-parliament, which meant parliamentary legislation. The Apology has been credited with being among the first portents of a crisis of authority between the king and Parliament. (This will be looked at later.)

Of more immediate consequence than the meeting of Parliament was the Convocation of Canterbury in 1604. A thorough review of the canons (the laws of the church) was undertaken. The new body of canons numbered 141, of which 97 were old and 44 were new. The more one analyzes the canons, both old and new, however, the more one realizes that the end product was not much more than a reaffirmation of the existing structure. The canons were reviewed by the king and issued under his own authority, not that of Convocation nor of Parliament. There were new canons and a new Bible, but the same old Church of England!

Puritanism was not the only religious issue James had to face. His innate sense of toleration led him to consider a new relationship with the Catholic church. He may well have been ready for a Hampton Court Conference on the possibilities of joining all Western Christendom in one great union, within which the pope could be the spiritual leader: *Primus Episcopas inter omnes Episcopas* (first among all the bishops) and also *Princeps Episcoporum* (the prince of bishops). All this was possible if the pope would "quit his godhead and usurping over kings." Pope Clement VIII thought James was on the verge of conversion to Rome. The queen, Anne of Denmark, was a Catholic and encouraged the idea that Prince Henry, the heir to the throne, would marry a Spanish princess. Nothing came of this for Henry or for his brother, Charles, later in the reign. James's sense of toleration would never let him go so far as to allow even the slightest possibility of restricting the full royal prerogative in religious matters. The hopes of Catholics had been raised high; James brought them low. The result was the Catholic Gunpowder Plot of November 5, 1605. Twenty barrels of gunpower were placed in the cellar of the Palace of Westminster to blow up the Houses of Parliament while James was there. Fortunately for James, if not for England, the plot was discovered and the perpetrators, including Guy Fawkes, were executed. To this day the "Guy" is hanged in effigy on November 5, the only continuing manifestation of the anti-Catholic passion that ran through English history for so many generations. James was as wary of opposition on the Catholic front as he had been on the Puritan front.

THE STRUGGLE
FOR SOVEREIGNTY

James I's reign and the period of Charles I's reign that preceded the Puritan Revolution are the years that scholars examine to determine the causes of the revolution. Some historians trace the causes back to Henry VIII and the fall of Cardinal Wolsey in 1529.[2] Some recent scholars have come close to saying that there may not have been any great, or at least any long-range, causes at all.[3] The whole matter of what caused the English or Puritan Revolution or Civil War is one of the great controversies in modern historiography, reaching beyond the field of English history itself into the wider fields of the history of revolution and the history of social change. The literature on the subject is vast. The remainder of this chapter will outline what appear to be the main issues and the main historical trends. Religion and the state will remain the central foci; most scholars agree that the events of 1640–1660 were largely, if not totally, about these matters.

James I had come to the throne of England following the momentus changes in church, state, and society associated with the reign of the Tudor dynasty. James presided over a society in which the "sovereign" powers were universally thought to be those of "king-in-parliament." The late-sixteenth-century French

---

2 Lawrence Stone, *The Causes of the English Revolution, 1529–1640* (New York: Oxford University Press, 1972).
3 Conrad Russell, *The Causes of the English Civil War* (New York: Oxford University Press, 1990).

politiques (who sought a "political" resolution of French religious strife) had become concerned with the definition and the substance of "sovereignty," and their ideas had already begun to spread into England. To the French, "sovereignty" meant the exercise of full power, above which there was nothing higher (at least not on earth). The English formula of "king-in-parliament" could also be expressed as the sovereignty of "king, lords, and commons." Whichever formula was used, the practical effect of such sovereignty was an act of Parliament, for only in such an act was the theory made manifest in action. When the three "estates" of the realm agreed upon a thing, that thing could become legally binding upon all subject to that sovereign authority.

The formula is still the basis of the British constitution to this day. There is no earthly limit as to what can be enacted into law by "king-in-parliament"; no court of law can set such a law aside on behalf of a higher law; there was and is no judicial review. Henry VIII said that he never stood higher in his authority than when he stood in Parliament. Such a system facilitates the taking of action; a government can really govern. All of this presupposes, however, that the three "estates" are in agreement. The problem arises when the three are not in agreement. The United States Constitution was deliberately designed to provide for these "checks and balances." The English (the British since 1707) have traditionally preferred an active system to an inactive one, which the American system can too easily become. The American system can result in gridlock. The history of seventeenth-century England is largely concerned with the struggles among the various contestants for the supreme power: the power to act in face of the opposition of either or both of the other claimants to power. The central issue, then, was a struggle for sovereignty; this in turn was countered by the search for political and religious liberty. The struggles over sovereignty, therefore, were completely entwined with the whole matter of religion.

The claimants for sovereign power were not the three estates as identified above. Rather, in chronological order, they were the king himself, the common law (as represented by Sir Edward Coke), and the House of Commons (once civil war had begun). Neither James I nor Charles I, at the beginning of his reign, thought of eliminating Parliament. Each just assumed that a "loyal" parliament would have no other wish than that of supporting the king in whatever he did (which was automatically assumed to be in the nation's interest). James lectured his parliaments on these matters and, after the first one, failed to work out a satisfactory relationship. Charles I was even more unbending than his father and after only two parliaments vowed never to meet with one again. The very fact that he was forced to back down and call the Long Parliament in 1640 was in itself a political defeat of the first magnitude.

The king's prerogative powers authorized him to act alone to defend the nation from enemies, foreign and domestic. His judgment was supreme, answerable to no one. The two Stuarts openly relied on the total acceptance by Parliament of what was a combination of Tudor practice and political theorizing. The theorizing seemed to many to take precedence over the more benign Tudor practice. The Tudors had arranged for their leading ministers to hold seats simultaneously in one or the other house. James failed to honor this custom and compounded his mistake by surrounding himself with Scottish favorites who were even more ignorant of English affairs than he was and whose claims to preferment seemed to have been based more on a pretty face than on administrative ability. The mistakes of the two Stuart kings had much to do with the outbreak of civil war and the Puritan Revolution. The destruction of the monarchy in 1649 was undone in 1660 at the Restoration, when the largely unreformed monarchy carried on under Charles II. It was to take a second revolution in 1688–1689 before the role of the king was more permanently defined.

Sir Edward Coke had become chief justice of the Court of Common Pleas in 1605, having been promoted to King's Bench by James as a way of removing him from involvement in cases that had political and constitutional ramifications. Coke was a remarkable man with untold influence on the course of English and, even more, American legal history. As Elizabeth's attorney-general he had been a supporter of the royal prerogative. As Speaker of the House of Commons, also under Elizabeth, he championed the rights of Parliament. As chief justice he championed the sovereignty of the common law. "The law is supreme and the law is what the judges say it is." (In other words, wherever Coke was is the place where power ought to be centered.) The sovereignty of the law is not the same thing as judicial review: the sovereign body of common law could not be repealed. This notion subordinated the role of the Parliament as well as that of the king. What did emerge from the theory, however, was the concept that part of the body of the common law was fundamental or superior in authority even if all of it was not. Americans, who learned their law from the twin volumes of Coke's *Institutes*, took up the idea of "fundamental" law when they wrote the American Constitution and created judicial review to accompany it.

The great rival to the king's claim to sovereign power came from the House of Commons after the Long Parliament had been in session for some months. There is no evidence that those who attended the opening sessions had any other ideas than the full acceptance of the sovereignty of the king-in-parliament. But the calling of the Long Parliament did not occur in a vacuum. It is necessary to summarize the history of the early Stuart reigns in some detail in order to see the mood each House and the king were in when the call for parliament came.

Those who see the early Stuart years as having all the necessary ingredients for the civil war and revolution that came forth in the 1640s often categorize the situation as being a conflict between "court" and "country." Both of these terms are only valid in the most general sense. This does not, however, mean that the use of these words is invalid. The "court" versus "country" dichotomy has a myriad of uses in explaining the struggle for sovereignty, as seen above. It also can be helpful in viewing the broader religious, economic, and social aspects of the background to conflict. The following brief description of the two camps will touch upon all of the various issues that distinguished each from the other.

COURT AND COUNTRY

The "court" of James I and of Charles I was itself a dynamic structure, changing over time, but always tending to be outside the mainstream of national life. Many names from the court of Elizabeth I are well known today: Leicester, Cecil, Walsingham, the Howards, and Drake, for example, all can be associated with some kind of positive contribution to the public good. The reigns of James and Charles have a different legacy. Raleigh was executed; Villiers or Buckingham was a tyrant; Strafford and Laud were the undoing of the king and kingdom. Francis Bacon was a great intellect but a corrupt lord chancellor; Sir Edward Coke was a great jurist and legal scholar, but in perpetual conflict with his king. The only statesman in the Elizabethan mold was Sir Robert Cecil, the earl of Salisbury, who tried to make the system work. In the end he was repudiated by both James and Parliament.

The image of the Jacobean court was of little men, often Scotsmen, advancing their own careers and fortunes at the expense of the English. The not-too-well-disguised sexual looseness of the court added to its negative image. The royal court and the church that it led and inspired were open to the charge of being unchristian. An increasingly puritanical moral code was developing in the country, and the immorality of the court and the low origins of many of its members increasingly divided the spirit of the court from the spirit of the country. The moral laxness was joined by financial profligacy. James thought he had inherited El Dorado and spent accordingly. He never understood or appreciated that Salisbury was trying to save him and his court from the wrath of ordinary Englishmen. Salisbury had conceived of "the Great Contract," whereby James would renounce certain outmoded and legally dubious sources of revenue in return for a permanent grant of tax money from Parliament. If adopted, the scheme might have prevented all of the turmoil of civil war and revolution. The scheme failed, however, because James wanted Parliament to act first, whereas Parliament wanted James to act first. It was already clear that the basic underlying trust that is necessary for any system to work without coercion was gone between James and Parliament. The lack of trust may have been largely personal at first; in time, however, it became institutionalized. James managed to retain some respect from the country; Charles I never did. When a king has to work at earning the respect of his subjects, the battle is already lost.

The "country" mentality was a loose composite of many dislikes of and frustrations with the state of English public life: the court's financial and sexual profligacy; the proliferation of titles and honors and the trappings of power for royal "favorites"; the king's failure to fight for England's honor in any of the phases of the Thirty Years' War, in which his own daughter was an injured party; the turning to the law courts for authorization of taxation, rather than turning to Parliament, as the "fundamental" law required. In the reigns of both James I and Charles I there was a growing disparity between the court's centralizing tendencies and the country's desire to retain local autonomy. Modern historians have tended to look with favor upon the early Stuart penchant for centralization of power because the poor benefited from such centralization through the developing system of poor relief. The central government also could influence the economy in ways that might benefit the nation as a whole rather than individual companies or regions. The "country" faction felt that it was the embodiment of the real England; it saw the court as being immoral and foreign. Charles I spent money on books for the library at Windsor and on paintings and painters; these pursuits were not welcomed by the "country." Royal cosmopolitanism and sophistication were seen as being degenerate and un-English.

The great cultural divide that separated the court and the country had its religious side. Most historians of seventeenth-century England now agree that the civil war and revolution were linked with Puritanism in one way or another. Efforts since the 1930s to precisely enumerate each religious position and assign each participant in the events of the 1640s and 1650s to one specific group have proven to be impossible. Because it is difficult to provide precise descriptions of the various Puritan factions, the following summary will endeavor to strike a balance between the general and the specific. Puritanism does have a certain body of beliefs and attitudes that are held in common.

Both in England and on the Continent, the seventeenth century began with a serious dispute within Protestant circles about the crucial matters of salvation: specifically, what role did God play and what role, if any, did the human being play? For the Christian who believed that this life on earth was nothing more than a preparation for the next, there could be no greater issue; it concerns the nature of life itself, not just the institution of religion. The dispute among Protestants had grown out of previous disputes between Catholics and the first Protestants in the early sixteenth century. All Christians agree that God makes the final decision about Heaven or Hell. The question that follows is whether or not the human being has any input. On the assumption that salvation is a zero-sum game, God either has 100 percent of the decision or he does not. Catholics believed in salvation by faith and good works; the latter at least left some option open to the individual conscience, which decided whether to partake of the sacraments or not. Those Protestants who were in the direct line of either Luther or Calvin were convinced that God alone made the decision and that the decision had in fact been made at the time he created the world—in other words, they believed in predestination. This belief stated that God was sovereign; any input from a human being was a derogation of and attack upon the divine sovereignty. In a nutshell, the Catholics said the human being had some role; the Calvinists insisted that the human had no role whatsoever. The Catholic position has been called "free will"; the Calvinist can be labeled either predestination or the sovereignty of God. From the Calvinist point of view the Catholic has denied the sovereignty of God, which was blasphemy. This was the issue that led Erasmus, the guiding spirit of the humanists and for many the spiritual father of Luther, to refuse to adhere to Lutheranism and to choose instead to remain a Catholic. For Erasmus the crucial issue was free will; it remained the crucial issue. Jacobus Arminius, the Dutch Protestant theologian, became the focus of the renewal of the great debate in early Stuart England. In the 1619 Synod of Dart, Arminius summed up his views: "God foreknew, but did not foreordain, who would be saved and who would be damned." Thus, salvation was not automatically predestined; "free will" had some scope.

"Arminianism" as an issue for historians has had a long and rocky course. Exactly how a theological issue could become the stuff of politics is difficult for those who live in the twentieth century to understand. Because of the lack of precision in so much Anglican theology, there is a corresponding lack of precision in the arguments over Arminianism. What was Arminianism? Who was an Arminian? What role did Arminianism play in the nation's life? Just as the issue of "free will" versus predestination would divide Catholics from Protestants in general, it also now came to divide Puritan, or reforming, Anglicans from those Anglicans who accepted the basic structure of the Church of England. A strict acceptance of predestination in the Calvinist tradition undermined the sacramental system and the clergy who performed those sacraments. The result was once again—no bishop, no king!

As the great debate over Arminianism moved on toward the calling of the Long Parliament in 1640, we can get a better grasp of the controversy by looking at the roles played by Charles I and William Laud, his bishop of London and later archbishop of Canterbury.

The Elizabethan Settlement of the church had resulted in a combination of largely Calvinist doctrine and a modified Catholic ritual. Along with this went the retention of the Catholic hierarchy of bishops, priests, and deacons, under the Lutheran structure of the royal governments. The great bones of contention for those who were called Puritans were the Catholic ritual and hierarchy. The true Calvinist was absolutely convinced that the Roman church was evil. Why would any true Christian want a church that retained any resemblance of this Satanic nature? These views had become prominent in the reign of Elizabeth, although they had become quiescent in the last years of her reign. James I's accession to the throne had raised the Puritans' hopes for reform; the Hampton Court Conference had dashed those hopes. The style, if not the substance, of James's reign had brought a broad opposition into being. The court had become identified with a narrowly denominational Anglicanism. There was no willingness to incorporate Puritan dissent within the church. The result was a fusion of the "country" and Puritan oppositions.

ARCHBISHOP LAUD

William Laud was bishop of St. David's in Wales at the accession of Charles I in 1625. Charles had become heir upon the death of his brother Henry in 1612. Laud quickly moved on to Bath and Wells, London, and Canterbury as each became vacant. He also became chancellor of Oxford University. He was, without question, a cleric after Charles's own heart. Charles himself was the first monarch to have been born and raised within the Church of England. Whatever the religious enthusiasm and beliefs of his predecessors may have been, they always treated the Church of England as being part of the political arena, as we have seen. This was not true of Charles. He was not only a Christian and a Protestant; he also was a true believer in the Anglican Church. Laud also was convinced that the Church of England as by law established was ipso facto God's church. He was determined to defend it and to enforce its rites and doctrines to the letter as well as the spirit of the law. How much he cared for or understood deeper and purer theological matters is debatable. The Church of England was God's and he and his king would use every effort and device at their command to carry out their divine commission.

Part of this view of religion was the belief that how things were done was as important as what was done. Laud was convinced that the ritual prescribed by law and the traditional Catholic ritual that preceded it were part of the divine plan for worship. Human beings had a duty to worship God and a duty to make the acts of worship as beautiful and uplifting as time and money would allow. Laud's scheme can be described in the simple words "the beauty of holiness." The full dramatic and ceremonial talents of the English people were to be devoted to the worship of God. The trouble was that "the beauty of holiness" smacked of a return to Roman Catholicism. Laud quickly got the reputation of being a secret Catholic and a tyrant.

Laud has been irrevocably linked with the Arminian movement. How much he may have thought about free will versus predestination is still questionable. But Arminianism in Puritan eyes meant a return to Catholicism; Laud's "beauty in holiness" also meant Catholicism. Laud and Arminianism were thus thrown together in the minds of the Puritans and both meant a Catholic (and Satanic) counterreformation. Laud was even suspected of having returned to the pope and being rewarded with the cardinal's red hat. The Puritans were not the only ones fooled by Laudianism. Even the pope thought that Laud was a potential convert. Laud and his king were committed Anglicans and no more. Laudianism, however, combined with King Charles's marriage to Henrietta Maria, the sister of King Louis XIII of France, could easily make anyone inclined toward a conspiratorial explanation of current events feel that there truly was a Catholic plot. Anglicanism was quickly becoming known as Laudianism. Puritanism, whatever else it may have been, was just as quickly becoming anti-Laudian. The willingness of Laud and the king to make use of the Court of High Commission to enforce religious conformity reinforced that old belief that Catholicism meant tyranny. Laud and Charles were playing with fire.

The differences between the Laudian/Arminian faction and the Puritan faction were not only those of ritual and doctrines of salvation. They also included differences over the basic life-style of the common person. The Anglican Church had retained the Catholic and medieval tradition of alternating between saints' days, which were times of feasting, and penitential days and weeks, which required fasting. Dozens of holidays were recognized until well into the nineteenth century. These holidays were celebrated with drinking, dancing, games, and dramas, and the general atmosphere was one of "reckless abandon" that the Puritans considered ungodly. The Puritans sought moderation and restraint in all things except the enthusiasm displayed for a good sermon. The sermon was itself one of the great issues dividing the two camps. The Anglicans stressed the proper execution of the elaborate rituals and the priest's role as a performer of the sacraments. Sinful humans may have been saved by Christ's death, but the salvation became efficacious for a particular person through a lively participation in the sacramental life of the church. To the Puritan, salvation was assured for the elect and all were anxious for signs as to who the elect might be. Some indications were the overall order and tone of the person's life and the degree to which Bible reading and listening to sermons expounding the truths of the Bible were a regular part of the person's life. All in all, the Anglican seemed to accept human nature and belief in a merciful God who would grant salvation to those who participated fully and joyfully in the ordinary life of the community and its parish church. The Puritan accepted restrictions on the pleasures of the flesh as signs that one was among God's chosen. The Anglican had in fact basically retained the Catholic assumption that humans were sinners by nature, but that salvation was possible through the forgiveness of sins by the church acting as God's surrogate. The Puritan was not interested in the forgiveness of sins, but in the prevention of the sinful acts in the first place. Anglicans could celebrate Christmas by getting drunk after a day of feasting and dancing. The Puritans celebrated it in church listening to the Bible and a long and learned sermon. The great attention that historians have paid to Puritanism during the past 150 years has undoubtedly resulted in our thinking that they represented the mainstream in English culture. This is not the case. The majority of the population of England was never Puritan. The Puritan triumph under Oliver Cromwell was, in the long haul, an aberration.

ANGLICANS AND PURITANS

That the Anglican-Puritan dispute might eventually result in civil war was beyond belief, except in retrospect. One of the issues that clearly separated the Anglican/Royalist faction from the Puritan/Parliamentary faction was the issue of church finance. The dissolution of the monasteries back in the 1530s had resulted in what was called the "impropriation of tithes," by which the monastic owner's right to appoint a priest to a living and the right to receive the tithes had been transferred to the new lay owner of the monastic estates. This lay control of so much of what had once been church property and church revenue was especially resented by Laud. Laud sought to take back into the hands of bishops as much of those impropriated revenues as possible, and he used the Court of High Commission to do so. Many Puritans were not opposed to the church increasing its revenues in order to provide for a more learned body of preachers. They were, however, opposed to the loss of lay property, often Puritan lay property, in order to enrich the episcopacy. That the deed was done through the prerogative courts, in opposition to the common-law courts, and with canon-law lawyers trained in the civil law of Rome rather than with common-law lawyers, inexorably led to the deep estrangement of those families and those interests that were linked together by the common law, parliamentary service, and a Puritan religious style.

It is useful to explore how the Puritan "style" differed from the Anglican because when the ultimate crisis did come, it was the Puritan/Parliamentary side that was willing to jettison the traditional English way and use force against the king and the church. In the introductory chapter there was discussion of the horizontal and the vertical approaches to religion and the relationship between the individual worshiper and the wider church. The early Stuart years saw this difference in attitude and style come to play a major role. The Church of England was the heir to the Catholic tradition whereby the church is both the body of believers and, at the same time, the body of ordained clergy who perform the sacraments. The Roman and Anglican churches are "communions" whereby the member or communicant is "in communion" with the bishop of his diocese, the priest under that bishop in that diocese, and the archbishops over the bishop. Beyond that, the Roman archbishop is in communion with the pope, whereas the Angelican archbishop is in a jurisdictional, if not a clerical, relationship with the king. One is a member of the larger group via a chain of hierarchical relationships. The actual taking of "communion" is a rite performed by the ordained for the benefit of the unordained. The rite is a "sacrament" in which a miracle is performed (according to the Roman Catholic) or something nonmiraculous but that looks miraculous is performed (according to the Anglican). For the Catholic the group to which one belongs is the worldwide Roman Christendom. For the Anglican the group is the English nation subject to its king.

For the Puritan the relationship with the church is horizontal. The believer's relationships are with fellow Christians who live and work in proximity to him or her. The church is the body of true believers and that body can be quite narrowly defined: the family, the extended family, the neighborhood, the village, the parish. The tie that bound the believers together was the "covenant," "covenants which come from the warmth of the heart and were bound with the steel of a will converted and conformed to God." Such a bond could not be on too large a level geographically since it assumed some intimacy of contact. Rather, the stress was on the local parish. This local dimension could in turn lead to separatism, which became a growing movement in the late sixteenth and early seventeenth centuries. It also led to the formation of the "independency" movement, which Oliver Cromwell was to represent. The "independent" congregations were still considered to be part of one nation. It was religious independence, not political separation. The very word "covenant" reeked with biblical meaning. It was easy for the convenanters to think in terms of having been "chosen," as distinct from being among the elect. Chosen or elected, those within the covenant were not just ordinary residents of a geographical area. The covenant was a symbol of one's separation from the mass of the people, not oneness with them. The two biblical sacraments of baptism and the Lord's Supper were regarded as "seals of the covenant-grace." They were not sacraments that transmitted grace. The covenanter was thus directly opposed to the fundamental basis of both the Catholic and Laudian Anglicanism, that sacraments did transmit grace.

The Separatism movement had begun when Robert Browne established a congregation at Norwich in 1580. It was soon condemned by the queen herself. No monarch could tolerate this movement. As long as the parish was a branch of the governmental structure, the separatism was tantamount to secession. The separatists sought a political as well as a religious independence. It is important to remember this essential import of separatism.

It is also important to distinguish between the royal attacks upon radical separatism and those upon the general Puritan movement. To reform the church from within was one thing; to secede from the established structure of government was quite another. This was a denial of the king's *potestas jurisdictionis;* perhaps it was a denial of his kingship. No bishop, no king, could also become "no parish, no king." It is useful to point out a little-noticed but significant fact about the emigrations to America. Jamestown was settled by those seeking economic rewards. Plymouth was founded by the Pilgrims, who were separatists and had gone to Holland before proceeding to America. The fact that James allowed them to go to America demonstrates the contrast between how the English and the French and Spanish handled dissent. England did not want dissenters at home and let them go to the colonies; France and Spain kept them at home and did not trust them to go to the colonies (at home, the king could at least keep an eye on them). The first Puritan settlement, Boston, was not established until Charles's reign. James I proved to be more tolerant of Puritans than Charles and Laud. Neither king, however, would tolerate separatism.

Besides the parish being a part of local government, the locus of power and the direction in which authority flowed (from top to bottom, or bottom to top) was also the issue that divided Anglican and Puritan on the question of whether or not the clergy should be more learned. The place of the clergyman in a society in which a majority were still illiterate is an exalted one. He was the natural leader of his community. The issue of whether he represented the community to the powers above or represented the king to the community below was crucial to the overall power structure. For the king there was only one right answer. This was an age in which the only means the king had to communicate with his subjects with any reasonable speed and accuracy was through the sermons given each Sunday in each parish. That required that the king control the bishops and the bishops control the priests. Members of the clergy who were less learned were more likely to be devoted to performing sacraments and delivering prescribed sermons than were the more learned clergymen of the Puritan cause, who were likely to have their own messages and the ability to give them well and with authority. They could use their sermons to cement their relationships with their congregants and forge a force of "independence" within the nation. This is what James meant by "no bishop, no king."

KING AND PARLIAMENT

Charles I had even more difficulty than James in dealing with his first parliaments. Charles was a more traditionally moral man than his father and was a good husband and a loving parent. He was a devout believer in the Church of England, as well as in his father's version of the "divine right" monarchy. Historians argue over whether or not Parliament was seeking greater power, in the last years of Elizabeth and the reigns of James and Charles. There were already sufficient grounds for a breakdown of trust between king and Parliament even if they sought nothing more than their traditional powers. The one great power Parliament did have was the right to determine whether or not taxes could be collected. The king had his age-old right to the revenues from the crown lands and to the customs duties. Besides these, he had certain court fees, wardship fees, and the like. Wardship and other leftovers from medieval feudalism had largely gone into abeyance before James I revived them. James also arbitrarily increased customs duties beyond the traditional amounts. A series of court cases fought over his fiscal rights had resulted in victories for the crown. Before Charles I ever came to the throne, there was the feeling among the people that something was fundamentally wrong. The king was increasing revenues more with the consent of his own appointed (and dismissable) judges than with the consent of Parliament. Charles continued the policy and brought it all to a head over the matter of ship money, the money paid by ports to help finance the navy.

The king claimed that his prerogative duty to defend the nation entitled him to collect ship money nationwide, not just in the ports. The ship money case of 1637 followed Charles's dissolution of his last parliament in 1629, at which time he said he would never call another into being. That declaration had in turn followed the signing by Charles of the Petition of Right of 1628, in which he had agreed to raise no new revenues without the consent of Parliament. The ship money decision, supporting the king's claim, marked the abandonment of the Petition of Right, the demise of Parliament, and the very real possibility that the new era of "personal rule" would be successful and would last forever. It would, in fact, last as long as the king could continue to raise the necessary revenues.

By the time Elizabeth I came to the throne, the ancient tradition that the "king must live of his own" was outdated. It was based on the principle that the king's government and the king's family should survive on those traditional revenues that were the king's by hereditary right. The later sixteenth century had seen the cost of government, even in peacetime, exceed the revenues from the traditional sources. The economic and social changes accompanying the Reformation had resulted in a larger government that did more things. The crown lands were very inefficiently managed, and although their proceeds doubled during the Tudor years, the cost of living quadrupled. Elizabeth resorted to the granting of monopolies and the sale of land to raise money. She also borrowed heavily and was in debt at her death. James resorted to extraordinary devices also, including the sale of titles, and even the creation of a new title, baronet, that was specifically for sale. That Charles needed money was understandable to students in later years; however, it was not understood by the parliaments of the later Tudor and early Stuart reigns. They always assumed that the crown's financial problems were caused by corruption, incompetence, and unnecessary wars. They were never willing to help out, except at a price that no king was willing to pay; namely, a reduction in his prerogative powers. That Parliament responded either by being negative or by putting forth ideas of their own on subjects of national interest, such as religion, is understandable. Whether Parliament was seeking to "win the initiative" or merely had an opportunity thrown their way is not all that crucial. The end result was the same.

The years from 1629 to 1640 saw the "personal rule" of Charles I. They also are known as the years of "thorough," the strict enforcement of the laws. "Thorough" was the epithet hurled at the regime dominated by the two "evil" advisers, Archbishop William Laud and Sir Thomas Wentworth, the earl of Strafford. Strafford had been among the opponents of the court during the early years of the reign. Charles invited him to join the government and he readily agreed to do so. His fellow country party colleagues assumed that he had been co-opted, which he undoubtedly had. Strafford was sent to Ireland to bring the island's chaotic administrative system into sufficient order so that more taxes than ever before could be collected and the sums not needed in Ireland itself could be sent to the court in London. The traditional policy that Ireland should pay for its own administration and, indeed, for its own conquest, had resulted in the failure to effectively conquer or administer the island. Strafford's charge, combined with his authoritarian personality, did not lead to fiscal surpluses, but they did lead to the unifying of disparate groups in Ireland in opposition to him. The king would have been better off if Ireland had remained disunited. The country factions back in England saw in Strafford the embodiment of their fears for the rights of Englishmen at home.

Strafford, Laud, and Ireland were to be joined by Scotland as the fourth side of the "coffin" that was being built for King Charles. The crisis that broke forth in Scotland was largely religious in origin. Before James I had ever gone down to England, the episcopal church structure, with bishops and dioceses, had been established. Prior to the 1630s it had generally been a paper structure as far as any impact upon Scotland's religious life was concerned. Charles I, the devout believer in the Church of England, decided that the Book of Common Prayer must be enforced in Scotland, as in England. This was intolerable in the eyes of most Scotsmen. Even those who were happy to accept English culture in general terms resented the imposition of an alien system under the overall guidance of a martinet like Laud. The results of Charles's decision were rebellion in Scotland and threats of war with the royal forces in England. Charles had actually begun his reign in Scotland by revoking the grants of church lands to laity that had occurred since the Reformation. He was threatening their property even before he threatened their church. The celebration of the Anglican communion service in St. Giles Cathedral in Edinburgh in 1637 was the last straw. The General Assembly met in 1638 and the Scottish parliament in 1639. Episcopacy was abolished, along with the use of the Book of Common Prayer. Charles refused to accept these acts of Parliament and tried to invade Scotland to enforce his will. The invasion was to be conducted by the English nobility serving at their own expense and with the help of the militias from the northern counties. The first Bishops' War (as it was called) quickly ended with the Pacification of Berwick in 1639.

Charles was urged to try again, but to first summon an English parliament and ask for money. If a parliament refused money, then he would be free to resort to extraordinary means of getting what he needed. This policy resulted in Charles calling the Short Parliament, which met from April 13 to May 5, 1640. It was at this time that the famous quote about the need to reduce "this kingdom" was attributed to Strafford and was leaked to an apprehensive world. Whether "this kingdom" meant Scotland, England, or Ireland has never been determined. All those who hated Strafford feared the worst. The Short Parliament accomplished nothing for the king, but it did give John Pym, a leading Puritan, a chance to express in an "eloquent oration" the accumulated frustration of a generation of country leaders. It was an excellent preparation for the Long Parliament that fall. Parliament was dissolved without granting a penny. The Scots crossed the Tweed River in August and camped in northern England at a cost of £850 per day, which they demanded that the king pay. Charles had failed to get money from Parliament but he also knew that he could no longer hope to raise money without Parliament. He was trapped. The new parliament was called for November 5, 1640. He could not rule without a parliament; he was soon to learn that he could not rule with one. Pym was ready, whether or not the king was.

THE LONG PARLIAMENT

The Long Parliament (the longest up to then) met at a point when the entire country could be said to be supporting the "country" opposition to the king. The support for the court in Parliament was negligible. John Pym and the great majority of the members of the House of Commons were determined upon reform. We now know that the distinction between Royalist and Parliamentarian had not yet developed. The distinction between Anglican and Puritan was also muted. If "court" meant Strafford and Laud, then almost everyone else was "country." It was the king's failure to cut his losses and remove these "evil advisers" that made civil war likely, if not inevitable.

Charles asked for taxes; Pym and the leadership had their own agenda: this parliament would not be dissolved without its own consent; parliaments in future should meet at least every three years; the prerogative courts would be abolished (except for Chancery); and Strafford and Laud would be impeached. Charles signed into law statutes on the first three items. Strafford and Laud were dealt with differently. Laud was placed in the Tower following indictment and was executed for treason in 1645. Strafford was impeached but the case against him was so obviously political rather than criminal that the trial was abandoned and he was condemned by act of attainder, which required no proof of crimes that would stand up in a common-law court. Charles in the end signed the bill of attainder and did not win popularity in spite of it. In fact, the opposition in Parliament treated him as though he were wounded and they should move in for the kill. Rather than winning points out of the necessary loss of his own key men, he lost even more respect. Charles was seemingly incapable of responding politically to a situation that was political in essence but that was also a fight for the sovereign power within the state and nation.

The passage of Pym's agenda and the removal of Strafford and Laud did lead some of the members of the Commons to feel some sympathy for the king and some regard for his position. Pym and his followers had accomplished their goals of reforming the structure of government and removing the evil advisers. However, Pym was convinced that Charles could not be trusted to honor the new system. Rebellion in Ireland, precipitated by Strafford's administration, brought the question of trust to the fore. Both king and country were in complete agreement that a rebellion in Ireland, assumed to be Catholic and anti-Protestant, must be crushed. Rumors spread through the land that the Catholics were massacring the Protestants. This was not true; the revolt was in fact interdenominational, although it soon became a Catholic revolt, but without massacres.

Agreement on raising an army to crush Ireland immediately led to disagreement over who should command it. What was soon to be called the Parliamentary party wanted the commander to be chosen by Parliament. What became known as the Royalist party wanted the king to play his traditional role as commander-in-chief. On this issue there was no agreement. Parliament declared its Militia Bill to be law in 1642 without the king's signature, calling it an "ordinance" since it was not a proper statute or act of Parliament. The gauntlet had been thrown down. Civil war was the result. It was to be some years before the new army raised by Parliament would fight the Irish. They had a war to win at home first. And win it they did!

THE CAUSES OF THE CIVIL WAR

Historians have argued for two generations over the causes of the civil war and/or revolution. There still is no consensus. It is easier to see who served on what side than it is to see why they did so. Within the House of Commons about 60 percent were Parliamentarians; the rest were Royalists. A study by D. Brunton and D. H. Pennington[4] showed that the differences between the two factions in the House of Commons were not economic, social, or religious but rather had more to do with service in and commitment to the Commons itself. The rival armies and their financial backers did make evident a divide separating the north and west from the south and east. The titled aristocracy and the Anglican clergy supported the king. The gentry were divided, with the north and west inclined toward the king and the south and east inclined toward Parliament. Religiously, the regions and the classes that might be inclined toward Puritanism were Parliamentarian. The average layman, especially in the rural areas, probably supported the king. Most of the country was probably the equivalent of a border area such as in the American Civil War. There was little sign of support for one side or the other in areas not already occupied by one or the other army.

Why, then, is the movement so frequently called the "Puritan Revolution"? The description is fully justified and it is necessary to examine the reasons why. The classic Victorian view was that the "Puritan Revolution" was a fight for political and religious liberty. The political side of the equation is irrevocably linked with the increased role sought and won by the House of Commons, by 1689 if not in the 1640s and 1650s. The religious side of the equation also has a focus. There was no search for twentieth-century-style religious toleration, for the church, if not the God, of your choice. Genuine belief in religious toleration was rare and hardly without limits. What the Puritans sought was a structure of church government that made local parish autonomy possible; they were not searching for individual choice. The Church of England and its Catholic predecessor

---

4 D. Brunton and D. H. Pennington, *Members of the Long Parliament* (Cambridge, Mass.: Harvard University Press, 1954).

were so structured that power flowed from the top down. The Puritans agreed that the flow should be upward, not downward. What the base from which the power would flow should be was not always agreed upon. The Presbyterian system of synods from the parish, county, provincial, and national levels would result in a national structure, which need not always be too solicitous of the views of the individual or the single parish. This was the Scottish system. King Charles abhorred it, and so did most English Puritans when they thought through all its implications. The English Puritan thrust was largely reflected in the structure that Oliver Cromwell would ultimately establish once he took power—a system that he called "independency" and later came to be called Congregationalism. The congregation, composed of the men of faith (the elect) in the neighborhood, would be bound together in a covenant and would worship God as God himself intended, in a form already outlined in the New Testament. Any further reliance upon the accumulated traditions of the past would have to be accepted by the individual congregation; nothing could be imposed from above, not by pope, not by king, not by bishop, not by synod. As the Puritan ascendency progressed through the 1640s and 1650s, some went so far as to assert that even leadership based upon book learning was wrong; to them, nothing should stand between the man of faith and God, not even knowledge based upon the study of the Bible.

Early in the opening session of the Long Parliament the Root and Branch Petition was received. The petition seems to have represented the views of the London mob that had organized on behalf of Burton, Bastwick, and Prynne, who earlier had been imprisoned for attacking Laud and his Arminian views. The release of Burton and Bastwick inspired the attack upon episcopacy, calling for its extirpation "Root and Branch." Such extreme demands eventually encouraged a basis of support for the king and the church, but not until the civil war began. The outbreak of civil war in 1642 alone is what finally determined who was on what side and what it was that inspired them. The alliance of the king and the Church of England was relatively easy to define and to accomplish. Just what linked all of the Puritan factions together remained difficult to determine. So much of what united them had been anti-Laudianism.

The Parliamentary military needs largely determined the initial rush to presbyterianism via the Solemn League and Covenant, the alliance with the Scots. The alliance implied that a victorious English Parliament would turn the Church of England into a Presbyterian church on the Scots model. As long as Scottish military support was needed, the full meaning was not brought home to those Englishmen who were religious independents at heart. Shortly before the signing of the covenant with Scotland, Parliament showed its colors on the matter of the Anglican communion service. It passed an ordinance calling for the rigid enforcement of a declaration issued in January of 1641 that ordered commissioners to be sent into every county "to demolish and remove out of churches and chapels all images, altars or tables turned altar-wise, crucifixes, superstitious pictures, and other monuments and relics of idolatry." The new ordinance went beyond this and called for the destruction of such items, which included communion rails, rood screens, pipe organs, fonts, and even the sacramental vestments. Before the Restoration of 1660, a great deal of damage was done to the interior art and architecture of the pre-Reformation churches. Even before the Church of England was officially abolished, vengeance was being wreaked upon it. The official abolition was itself to come about in various stages.

In 1643 the traditional powers-that-be in the local churches sent representatives to the Westminster Assembly of Puritan Divines, or leaders. Once they arrived it was clear that presbyterianism was in the ascendency. A new Westminster Confession was composed in place of the Anglican catechism. Episcopacy was formally abolished by Parliament and a new Directory was composed to replace the Book of Common Prayer. Archbishop Laud was executed for treason in January of 1645 and for all practical purposes the Church of England was gone. No one statute had abolished the Church of England, but it had been done incrementally. The Directory that replaced the Book of Common Prayer had dropped five of the sacraments, retaining baptism and the communion service, but in a purely Calvinist mold. The abolition of episcopacy, combined with the rejection of the Prayer Book, effectively stripped the church of all that made it Anglican. The supreme governorship of the king was, of course, a dead letter anyway as far as Parliament was concerned.

But presbyterianism was not to be the victor in the struggle for the religious control of England. The English presbyterians and the Scots with whom they were now allied still tended to think in terms of a national church structure. The structure might be the direct opposite of the Anglican episcopal system, but whether the national church was to have power flowing from the top down or from the bottom up, a national church was still regarded as being inconsistent with the covenanting of a single congregation. The whole point of stressing a single congregation was to deny the place for national structure. The religious enthusiasm of the members of the newly created New Model Army that would soon lead Parliament to victory over the king and the simultaneous demise of the alliance with the Scots made the future more hospitable for these supporters of independency. Cromwell was their leader as well as a military and national leader.

Historians have argued for years over whether or not the civil war was the result of a revolutionary urge or instead precipitated that revolution. Whichever view one holds, the sequence of events gives some clues. The "Civil War" is often divided into two parts: 1642–1646 and 1648. The first civil war was fought by a parliament elected in 1640 on a traditional franchise with no thought of either civil war or revolution. It sought only to restore a system whereby the king would honor the age-old customs as the country interpreted them. That meant a government that actually did little on a local level. The king should "live of his own" financially and turn to Parliament when he could not. The church should maintain the integrity of the link between God and man and allow each parish to continue its traditional style of worship. For most parishes that meant some form of Anglicanism. As long as Catholics kept quiet and stayed away from the public eye, there was no great public interest in enforcing the recusancy laws requiring Catholic attendance at Anglican Church services. All in all the nation was not in a mood for dramatic change. However, the king and his evil advisers, who were viewed as the instigators of change, were problems. The Long Parliament passed a series of reforms designed to restore and to maintain the traditional system. The king's attempt to impose Anglicanism upon Scotland, his attempt to create a system of "thorough" government in both Ireland and England, and his use of various devices to acquire extra revenues through the consent of the courts rather than of Parliament unified the country (and parliamentary) leadership in a determination that the rot had to stop. Added to this growing alienation of the Stuart court from the country was the increasing public apprehension over the royal family itself.

The Grand Remonstrance of December 1641 and the Nineteen Propositions of June 1642, following the outbreak of war in April 1642, called for the king's children to be educated by tutors appointed by Parliament. Nothing could more clearly demonstrate the total collapse of trust. No father could submit to such demands. The total breakdown was more a failure on the part of persons than of institutions. But the English constitution had not as yet made provision for such a breakdown; the king was still in theory and in fact responsible for the governance of the kingdom. Once the evil advisers were gone, the opposition had to either submit to the king or remove the king. No one could think of an intermediary measure. It was not until 1688–1689 and the Glorious Revolution that solutions for the problem were found. The causes of the crisis of the 1640s and 1650s were both complex and simple. Where does responsibility (sovereign power) rest when the king, the House of Lords, and the House of Commons cannot agree? The outbreak of war brought to the surface a host of party, regional, class, denominational, and intellectual conflicts. For some historians this, and not the fight against the king, was the true revolution.

ENGLAND AT WAR

The Parliamentary army initially was led by members of Parliament and their protégés. The king's army, man for man, was probably better suited for battle, relying as it did upon men more used to riding and to leading soldiers on countryside expeditions. In early 1645 Cromwell secured the passage of the Self-

Denying Ordinance, which removed members of the House of Commons from the army, except for Cromwell himself. The New Model Army was to be composed of and led by God-fearing Christians with skills commensurate with the task before them. This was a truly remarkable force. It not only won its battles and captured the king within the year, but it also supplied from within its own ranks men whose ideas provided the basis for a new system of government and a new society. More time and effort went into giving and hearing sermons than was the case throughout most of the Crusades of the Middle Ages. The chaplains became so important to the ordinary soldiers that future armies have put chaplains in the officer corps and given them less intimate contact with the troops, so as not to undermine the authority of the military leaders. The chaplains were the natural leaders of the common soldiers, but they often had ideas that were out of step with those of Cromwell and his fellow officers, ideas more anti-authority and anti-elite than those of the more traditionally minded officers. Cromwell had created this army and was proud of it. In the fall of 1645 he wrote the following description to Lenthall, the Speaker of the Commons:

> It may be thought that some praises are due to these gallant men, of whose valor so much mention is made: their humble suit to you and all that have an interest in this blessing, is, that in the remembrance of God's praises they may be forgotten. It's their joy that they are instruments that God vouchsafes to use them. Sir, they that have been employed in this service know that faith and prayer obtained this city [Bristol] for you. I do not say ours only, but of the people of God with you and all England over, who have wrestled with God for a blessing in this very thing. Our desires are, that God may be glorified by the same spirit of faith by which we asked all our sufficiency, and having received it, it's meet that He have all praise. Presbyterians, Independents, all had here the same spirit of faith and prayer; the same pretense and answer; they agree here, know no names of difference: pity it is it should be otherwise anywhere.[5]

---

5 "Letter from Cromwell, dated from Bristol, 14 September 1645," Stuart E. Prall, ed., *The Puritan Revolution: a Documentary History* (New York: Anchor Books, 1968), pp. 124–125.

The defeat of King Charles I in 1646 and his imprisonment was followed by useless negotiations with him and his own plotting with the Scots. He promised to establish the Presbyterian structure in England if the Scots would help him. The king's escape from Hampton Court Palace and the resumption of the civil war, this time with Scotland on the king's side, resulted in defeat for Charles, for Scotland, and for presbyterianism as well. Colonel Pride's Purge, with Cromwell's approval, of the House of Commons in 1648, prior to the trial and execution of the king, eliminated all those suspected of complicity with the king in the second civil war. The remaining rump of the House of Commons (the part still sitting) was down to a little over a hundred members out of the five hundred originally elected in 1640. All of them were religiously what we would now call Independents (Congregationalists) or Baptists. This body attempted to try the king for treason according to traditional common-law procedures, but they failed. Treason was a crime against the king; the king could not commit treason. He is above the law as a person. Without a proper trial the king was found guilty and was sentenced to death. His execution sent a shock wave through England and throughout Europe. The supreme moment on the revolutionary agenda was always the moment that sealed its fate. The king's trial and death were to be victories for the Royalists in the not-so-long run. The day of the execution, January 30, 1649, the House of Commons also formally abolished the monarchy itself and the House of Lords. The Church of England was already gone. Nothing but the House of Commons, and it a mere rump, represented continuity with the ancient constitution.

THE INTERREGNUM, 1649–1660

Several efforts were made over the years following the first capture of the king (1646) to draw up a written constitution to replace the now defunct unwritten one. The chaplains and enlisted men of the New Model Army produced various versions of The Agreement of the People. While they prepared their various drafts, the officers issued their own Heads of the Proposals. Both constitutions provided for religious freedom or toleration for all believing Christians; The Heads of the Proposals denied toleration to Roman Catholics and also prohibited the use of the Book of Common Prayer, which effectively outlawed Anglicanism as well. With these exceptions to religious freedom, the proposal also stated that no one could be forced to take the covenant or to subscribe to any particular statement of religious beliefs. The Agreement of the People called for religious freedom and for the new government to encourage the preaching and the practicing of the true Christian life and faith. However, it too declared that none of these calls for religious toleration applied to supporters of the popes or prelates ("prelates" included the ordained clergy of the Church of England). The new religious dispensations, as proposed in the last years of the Long Parliament, did grant toleration to Christians, but limited to those calling themselves Independents, Baptists, and (later on) Presbyterians (as long as the Presbyterians were not seeking to impose a state church). Under Cromwell the individual parishes were prohibited from using the Prayer Book and its rituals. Each parish could conduct simple services according to the usage of the Baptists, Independents, Congregationalists, or the Presbyterian churches. Each parish was subject to the local and national political authorities. Christmas was no longer recognized as a holiday; births, marriages, and burials were considered to be secular events in a person's life. The traditional Prayer Book liturgy could not be used for these "rites of passage."

Following Cromwell's forcible dissolution of the rump of the Long Parliament in April 1653, the supreme legislative power was given by Cromwell to the Nominated (appointed), or Barebone's (Praise-God Barebone was a member) Parliament. It actually enacted nothing of consequence and was soon viewed with horror by Oliver Cromwell and his officers. Among their attempted acts was one to abolish the common law. Cromwell and his officers spent the fall of 1653 putting together the one and only written constitution in English history—the Instrument of Government of 1653 which replaced the nominated Parliament. This document made Oliver Cromwell lord protector of the united British Isles. The Commonwealth (1649–1653) was replaced by the Protectorate (1653–1658). This unification had already been accomplished by Cromwell and his New Model Army. Article XXXVII provided the following:

That such as profess faith in God by Jesus Christ (though different in judgment from the doctrine, worship or discipline publicly held forth) shall not be restrained from, but shall be protected in, the professions of the faith and exercise of their religion; so as they abuse not this liberty to the civil injury of others and to the actual disturbance of the public peace on their parts: provided this liberty be not extended to Popery or Prelacy, nor to such as, under the profession of Christ, hold forth and practice licentiousness.[6]

OLIVER CROMWELL

Oliver Cromwell was undoubtedly the ablest person to rule seventeenth-century England. Cromwell was a landowner of moderate wealth in Huntingtonshire. He first entered Parliament in 1628—the year of the Petition of Right—but played no active role. In 1638 he claimed to have had a "religious experience" when he was "being given to see the light." Not until the outbreak of civil war did he become a figure of consequence on the national scene. He was to prove himself to be a man of great military and political talents, a born leader who could make the toughest decisions in the face of the greatest obstacles. He was later seen as the "English Napoleon Bonaparte." He was also a true believer in the Protestant, Calvinist, Puritan God. Added to these traits was a genuine commitment to political and religious liberty. Cromwell believed in the very same causes that nineteenth-century historians assumed led to the Puritan Revolution in the first place, the need for political and religious liberty. Cromwell was then and has often since been seen as a hypocrite. Perhaps he was, but that was not how he saw himself. Cromwell assumed that once he had executed the king, free elections according to the traditional franchise would elect a Royalist parliament. The response from the crowd at the execution of the king convinced him of that. True religious freedom would mean the return of the Book of Common Prayer and the priests, if not the bishops, because the majority of the people were Anglican. Cromwell hoped that time, and not too much of it at that,

---

6 Ibid. p. 261.

would eliminate the remnants of the old political and religious persuasions and the new persuasions would command a majority without the need for coercion. Time was not Cromwell's friend; he died in 1658, before such a day ever came. The old system was restored soon thereafter.

THE LEVELLERS, THE DIGGERS, AND THE FIFTH-MONARCHY MEN

The short life of the Barebone's Parliament was marked by the appearance of many radical religious sects who joined the emerging radical political and social groups in spite of the care Cromwell took in selecting the membership. The most famous of the latter were the Levellers and the Diggers, who sought to move the new constitutional settlement towards expanding the franchise and creating a society in which rights and dignity for all would replace the age-old class structure that had been such a hallmark of English life. The Levellers sought social equality, but not political equality. Voting rights would be given to all men who were not servants, but the word *servant* included all who worked for a wage. The Levellers were strongly represented in the army and in the Nominated Parliament. The Diggers were the followers of Gerrard Winstonley and advocated a rural communion, or the communal ownership of the land. They were few in number and had little political influence. The Diggers called themselves the "true levellers" and got their own name from the song: "You noble Diggers all, stand up now, stand up now...." Every century or so has seen a major movement devoted to forceful elimination of a class structure. All such efforts at a sudden transformation have been marked by failure. Cromwell himself, a traditional supporter of the class structure, saw to the defeat of the Levellers and their leader, John Lilburne. The religious radicals were most clearly represented by the Fifth-Monarchy Men. They believed that the four great monarchies in the Book of Daniel—the Assyrian, the Persian, the Greek, and the Roman—were now at an end. They saw the Church of England as the last gasp of the "Roman" monarchy, and they believed that the fifth monarchy would be the kingdom of Jesus Christ on earth and that it was soon to come. The day was at hand and all that was needed was one last violent push. Cromwell crushed their one rebellion in 1657, and as an organized group they did not outlive him. They were, however, symptomatic of a great swell of resentment against the world as it was. There did not seem to be any more true Christian community spirit under Cromwell's Protectorate than there had been under the old Church of England. These radical groups could all agree that "new presbyters were but old priests writ large." Many people found that the Puritan dream of a more highly educated clergy had wrought no improvement, which led to a general attack on religious learning. The masses came to believe that the true faith would shine forth from the brow of the true Christian as a light coming forth from the real inner source—God's grace. No learning should get in its way.

THE MAJOR-GENERALS

Besides the opposition from the radicals on his left, Cromwell faced opposition from those who had been Royalists and/or Anglicans and who refused to accept the new dispensation as permanent in either church or state. To consolidate control over the whole country, Cromwell divided England into twelve districts, each under the overall command of a major-general. These officials were given the equivalent of martial-law authority and could use it with impunity to stamp out political and religious dissent. The independent congregations that became the hallmark of the Cromwellian religious system had hitherto allowed a certain religious toleration (each congregation or parish could choose to conduct services in the Presbyterian, Baptist, or Independent style). Although the Book of Common Prayer could not be read, it could still be recited from memory. The major-generals were determined to wipe out all such threats to the new unity. People were encouraged to spy on their relatives and neighbors and to report on their activities. Anglican forms of worship, as well as dancing, gambling, card playing, and excessive drinking, were all subject to arrest and punishment. Within the year 1655 Cromwell removed the major-generals because of vast public revulsion to their presence, but his regime would be called a military dictatorship by most Englishmen ever since, and their tenure made the very word "republic" a pejorative term. Restoration of monarchy was in the air for the remainder of Cromwell's life and that of the Protectorate. There was even the suggestion that Cromwell might have accepted the crown as a compromise; a Cromwellian crown if not a Stuart one. The Humble Petition and Advice of 1657 did restore a second legislative chamber, however, but not the crown.

Oliver Cromwell died in September 1658 and was succeeded by his elder but unworthy son, Richard. In January 1659 Richard called for the election of a new parliament under the Protectorate. In April of 1659 he was forced by the army officers to dissolve it and he himself went into retirement from the political area. The army recalled the rump of the Long Parliament and then dismissed it. The army leaders, especially General George Monck in Scotland, decided that the days of the politicians were over. Monck recalled the rump, as well as all of the Presbyterians expelled at Pride's Purge in 1648. This body in turn dissolved itself, according to the statute passed at the beginning of the Long Parliament and signed by Charles I. A new parliament was called under the traditional prerevolutionary franchise in April 1660. The traditional franchise allowed voting rights to the forty-shilling freeholders in the counties. Each borough had its own rules, but generally the franchise was limited to either landowners or businessmen within the borough. A few boroughs had universal manhood suffrage. Meeting as a "convention" because it was not called by a king, the parliament arranged for the arrival of the new king, Charles II. The new king had gone into exile in France after his father's defeat. He later had set up a court-in-exile in Holland in anticipation of being restored to the English throne. He was not invited back. His right to rule was assumed; only the place and date of his arrival from Holland had to be negotiated. The Interregnum was over.

6 / RESTORATION AND GLORIOUS REVOLUTION

Before sailing for England in May 1660 Charles II issued the Declaration of Breda, which called for tolerance and forgiveness. He would punish no one for their past deeds against him and his father unless Parliament itself would name the names. This generosity was not a mere political calculation. Charles II was closer to his grandfather than to his father in many ways. There was no question that he would be a "divine right" monarch in things political and administrative if that were possible. In religious matters, he was determined to preserve his place as supreme governor of the Church of England, but that church could be reformed. Charles and his chief minister, Lord Chancellor Clarendon, were both willing to restructure the church in liturgy at least, so that the church could come closer to being what its name implied—the church of all (or most) English people. Laud had made the Church of England one denomination among many, but the only denomination that was allowed to operate. The newly elected Convention of 1660 was a mixture of Anglicans and Puritans. It chose to postpone the new dispositon until the election of a regular parliament. The general election of 1661 returned a parliament that was overwhelmingly Anglican. This parliament lasted until 1679 and has been called the Long Parliament of the Restoration or the Cavalier Parliament. Because "Cavalier" is a term that refers to an adherent of Charles I, the latter name summarizes the strong Anglican and Royalist orientation that was reflected in its work.

As the years went by, the gap that separated the new king from his Lord Chancellor Clarendon became clearer, as did the gap between the king and his parliament. The nature of the Restoration settlement had a lot to do with the divergent views taken by different groups and different persons. The king had all his

powers and estates restored as they had been up to the veto by
Charles I of the Militia Bill in 1642. The Church of England had
all its property restored, but some of the Puritans who had become holders of parishes during the Commonwealth and the
Protectorate managed to retain them by taking the new oaths of
allegiance. Many formerly expelled Anglican clergy had been
badly treated during the revolutionary era. Some had even been
sent into the cane fields in the Caribbean. They certainly did not
return with hearts inclined toward forgiveness. The aristocracy
had their titles restored, but only a few got lands back. Any
lands that had been sold to get money for Charles I were not restored. Lands that had been sold to pay fines to the Cromwellian
authorities were not restored. The same was true for the property of the gentry. Charles II sought tolerance; no one else did.
Clarendon also expected the king to govern with the cooperation
of the lord chancellor and the Privy Council. Charles II did not
welcome any restraints on his personal autonomy. Thus the king
was not always at one with Parliament, or the church, or his lord
chancellor.

THE RELIGIOUS SETTLEMENT

The religious settlement comprised a series of acts, called the
"Clarendon Code," passed over a five-year period. However,
Clarendon did not support the code, nor did the king, even
though he chose to sign each one into law. Clarendon, as lord
chancellor, was irrevocably associated with them in name at
least. The first was the Corporation Act of 1661, which denied
election to municipal councils to anyone who did not renounce
the Solemn League and Covenant of 1643, refused to receive communion in the Church of England, or refused to take an oath of
nonresistance to the king as supreme governor of the church.
Municipal corporations supposedly would be solidly Anglican
from now on. The members of Parliament elected by these corporations would also be loyal Anglicans, it was assumed by
those supporting the act.

The Act of Uniformity followed in 1662. Beyond a few minor
changes in wording, the new Book of Common Prayer that it authorized was the same as that of 1559, and was to be followed

without any exceptions either as to persons or provisions. Also under the act no one could hold a church living who was not an ordained Anglican priest, and no one could be a tutor, teacher, or professor without the permission of the diocesan bishop. For all practical purposes Laudianism had triumphed. The Church of England was to be the one and only church allowed to practice. There was no doubt that Parliament knew what it was doing and knew what it wanted. Those who dissented from the church, such as the old Puritans, the new Quakers, or the old Roman Catholics, were to be denied an opportunity to worship in public and roles in local or national government. Charles II signed the act but quickly responded with a Declaration of Indulgence granting dispensations to Catholics and dissenters, if Parliament approved. It did not.

The remainder of the code followed in short order. The Conventicle Act of 1664 stated that no clergyman deprived of his living by the Act of Uniformity could preach to more than five persons at a time. Also, no secret places of worship were to be honored. In 1665 the Five-Mile Act further restricted the deprived clergy by prohibiting them from going within five miles of the parish from which they had been expelled. All of this was signed into law by the king, but his heart was not in its enforcement.

THE TEST ACT

In 1672 Charles II again issued a Declaration of Indulgence. This time Parliament not only refused to accept it, but countered with the passage of the Test Act of 1673. This was worded so as to make it perfectly clear what was acceptable and what was not. The "test," receiving communion in the Church of England, had to be passed by anyone serving in an office of "trust or profit" under the crown, anyone who held a fellowship at Oxford or Cambridge, or even by anyone who might receive a degree from either university. It also barred anyone who did not pass the test from holding a commission in the army or navy and, of course, from positions within the Anglican Church itself.

The king had little choice but to sign the bill into law, partly because his own religious convictions were beginning to be the talk of certain elements in the country and in Parliament. The secret Treaty of Dover actually contained a provision calling for Charles to convert to the Catholic religion, at a time of his own choosing, which is why Charles wanted the treaty kept secret (he waited until he was on his deathbed before accomplishing the conversion). The subsidy that Charles received from France and Louis XIV was known. The atmosphere at court struck many as being pro-French and pro-Catholic. Charles did in fact practice religious tolerance and was himself pro-Catholic. He also was determined to get his hands on as much money as possible without having to compromise with Parliament to get it. Louis's terms were easier, only requiring his eventual conversion to Catholicism and assistance in a war against Holland. By forcing Charles to sign the Test Act into law, the English state, along with its armed forces and the ancient universities, was to be totally wedded to the Anglican establishment. This was to remain the law, however rigorously or loosely enforced, until 1828.

THE EXCLUSION CRISIS

The great crisis of Charles II's reign was the dispute over the succession to the throne with the attempts to "exclude" James. Charles's brother and heir was James, the duke of York. James was a Catholic and had taken as his second wife a Catholic, Mary of Modena. By his first wife, Lady Anne Hyde, Clarendon's daughter, he had two daughters, Mary and Anne, both raised as Protestants and both to be married to Protestants. As long as James was a widower with two Protestant daughters there was little to fear from his succession. But his remarriage to a Catholic raised the specter of a son who could become a Catholic heir. These doubts about the succession combined with panic about a so-called Popish Plot, talk of which was spread by the infamous liar Titus Oates. Even though in fact there was no plot, the nation was gripped with fear. James and his wife were known to be in contact in some way or another with the French court and, even though James's patriotism cannot be challenged in retrospect, the public feared the worst: that their king would be removed for the benefit of a Catholic successor in league with the Jesuits and the French. A worse combination could not be imagined.

The Exclusion Crisis was the result of all these fears. Charles dissolved Parliament and called for new elections. Between 1679 and 1681 there were three general elections, each electing a House of Commons determined to remove James from the throne by one device or another. The leader of the opposition to the king was the earl of Shaftesbury, who had earlier served in the administration forever known as the CABAL. (From 1667–1673, Charles's chief advisors had been Clifford, Arlington, Buckingham, Ashley [Shaftesbury] and Lauderdale. The acronym, CABAL, is taken from the first letters of their names.) Some in Parliament wanted James to be king but with a Protestant regent. Some wanted Mary to be queen in place of her father. Others, including Shaftesbury, wanted the crown to go to Charles's beloved but illegitimate son, the duke of Monmouth. This was all beyond anything that Charles would himself contemplate. Even though Charles did not like James nor his taste in women, he was himself a firm believer in the divine nature of hereditary monarchy. And James was the heir by birthright.

WHIGS AND TORIES

These elections to three consecutive parliaments were the first ones fought on something resembling modern party lines. Those favoring exclusion of James became known as the Whigs, and the opponents of exclusion were the Tories. The two camps could trace their ancestry back to the Puritan Revolution. The Whigs were heirs to the Puritan and Parliamentary traditions, and the Tories were the heirs to the Royalist and Anglican traditions. Each party had been given its name by the other party: "Whigs" were really being called Scottish horse thieves by the "Tories," who in turn were being called Irish cattle thieves by the Whigs. Each "party" had an organization and introduced real issues of national import into the local parliamentary elections, where purely local issues and persons usually dominated. The two parties also clearly advocated different political principles. The Whigs believed in hereditary monarchy, except in an emergency, at which time Parliament could be seen as the true embodiment of the nation and could legislate an alternative. Whigs also were Anglicans, or else they could not engage in politics, but they might have Puritan or dissenting origins, or they might even have been Dissenters, if not for the Test Act. Once the restored church had rejected reform, those who had been Puritans were either to become regular Anglicans or were to "dissent" from the established church. Tories believed in heredity monarchy under all circumstances (although 1688–1689 was to disprove this), as well as in the Church of England as by law established. During the Exclusion Crisis, the Whigs wanted Parliament to save the nation from a Catholic king. The Tories wanted to consolidate the principles of hereditary succession and the Anglican principle of nonresistance to established authority.

Exclusion failed and its leader, Lord Shaftesbury, was ruined politically. The country had come close to civil war; Charles and Shaftesbury each gambled on the fear of such a war. Shaftesbury thought the fear of war would force the king to back down. Charles thought the nation preferred stability and would blame the Whigs for creating a potential civil war. Charles read the mood correctly. The nation did blame the Whigs, and James was to keep his position as heir. The ultimate irony was that as a Catholic, James had to resign as lord high admiral and had to vacate his seat in the House of Lords. The only job still open to him was the kingship itself.

THE ACCESSION OF JAMES II

Charles II died in 1685 and James acceded to the throne with a good deal of public relief, not because he was a Catholic, but because his accession occurred peacefully and lawfully. The nation was indeed sick of civil wars. The new king, a Catholic married to a Catholic, had two Protestant daughters. Many in the know thought that James was too old and unhealthy to produce a male heir; at least most hoped that he would not. James proclaimed his determination to preserve the Church of England as by law established. He was rewarded with the election of the most heavily Tory parliament yet seen. It in turn voted him a permanent tax-based income greater than that given to any of his predecessors. He had to face a Protestant rebellion against a Catholic king, led by Monmouth, which was easily crushed in the west, followed by a savage vengeance. In Scotland he was faced with the Argyll rebellion, also by Protestants, which also failed. While governing Scotland for his brother, James had earned the hatred of many Scottish Protestants. In England his accession coincided with the revocation of the Edict of Nantes in France by Louis XIV. This canceled the last measure of tolerance that had been granted the French Huguenots. The flow into England of skilled Huguenots fleeing persecution quickly led many in England to fear for the worst from the Catholics. The nation was grateful to have had a peaceful succession to the throne but it was wary of what the short-term consequences might be while he still lived. An aging king with Protestant heirs was not a long-range threat, however.

A CATHOLIC KING

Historians in the years since World War II have argued over just what James sought to achieve in the area of religion. He himself claimed that he would defend the Church of England "as by law established." He also said that he sought to establish the Roman Catholic religion and to offer toleration to the Dissenters. Just what "establishment" and "toleration" meant was not understood by the great mass of the English people then (and is still not understood today). Some historians maintain that he sought nothing more than the "establishment" of the Roman church as one among many churches, sharing this toleration with the Dissenters. For most historians, however, this view seems to be anachronistic, imposing twentieth-century toleration upon the seventeenth century, where it really does not apply. Nothing in James's actions gives credence to such an interpretation. On the contrary, in Scotland at the time of the Exclusion Crisis he treated the Protestants harshly. His attempts to woo the Dissenting leaders into cooperating with him in his quest for the repeal of the Test Act went largely unanswered, except for William Penn, the Quaker and future governor of Pennsylvania, who was a great friend of James, as his father, Admiral Penn, had been in earlier years.

James was convinced, correctly, that even the most Tory of parliaments would not repeal the Test Act nor condone the "establishment" of Roman Catholicism. He spent the remainder of his reign in a series of futile attempts to restructure the franchise so as to secure the election of a House of Commons bent on repeal and toleration. Once he dissolved his initial parliament, no parliament met again in his reign, since no possible combination of members under the traditional franchise would be willing to cooperate with him, the great majority of those already enfranchised being Anglican. One reason why James failed in his wooing of dissenters was the clever politicizing done by some of the Anglican clergy.

On one occasion James followed Charles's example and resorted, temporarily, to another Declaration of Indulgence in April 1687. This followed the king's victory in a collusive court case, Godden vs. Hales, in which the king was declared to have the right to dispense with the Test Act and to appoint Catholic officers to his army in London. The declaration also provided for the creation of a new Court of High Commission comparable to the one abolished by the Long Parliament. James also attempted to override the statutes of Magdalen College at Oxford University and appoint a Catholic master. All of these acts were viewed as being extralegal, if not illegal, by the Anglican leaders. The Dissenters were put to the test themselves. Would they rather receive toleration illegally from a Catholic king who could not be trusted, or from a Tory/Anglican parliament that might well grant toleration in the future and by strictly legal means? When put this way, it is perhaps understandable that the Dissenting leaders went along with these offers of future relief rather than the king's offer of instant relief. If James were indeed a man of toleration, he was certainly an incompetent presenter of his case.

THE DECLARATION OF INDULGENCE TRIAL

For James the year 1687 ended on a note of triumph. The queen was pregnant. The birth of a son would secure the future for James's policies. James's opposition was soon forced to make plans for that future. Given James's age and health, there were doubts about his ability to father a child. Now there were doubts as to the child's true paternity, although no one really doubted the queen's honesty. That James seemed convinced that the baby would be a boy was taken by some as proof that something in the nature of a plot was developing. As the months went by, James was emboldened to again call for the enforcement of his earlier Declaration of Indulgence. In May of 1688 he called upon the bishops to see that the declaration was read out in each parish church in the land. This declaration was illegal in the eyes of the bishops, and the king was ordering them to join in breaking the law by requiring it to be read. Seven bishops refused to do so and signed a petition, which was carried to James. The king was furious and brought about indictments for criminal libel against them, on the grounds that by refusing his command they were accusing the king of ordering an illegal act. The seven, including William Sancroft, the archbishop of Canterbury, were imprisoned in the Tower. A jury was carefully picked to hear the case. Many ordinary citizens of London staged a demonstration on behalf of the seven in the Tower. This was truly a unique occasion. Whatever may have been the commitment of the ordinary people to the Church of England, bishops, individually and collectively, had never been popular figures. James should have been worried, not just annoyed, by such a demonstration.

THE BIRTH OF AN HEIR

Before the trial was completed the queen gave birth to a baby boy, James Francis Edward, prince of Wales. The king was overjoyed. The nation was largely apprehensive, if not actually suspicious. Rumors spread about the "warming pan incident": it was easier for the believer in hereditary monarchy to assume that the baby was an imposter than it was to withhold allegiance from that baby. Many quickly became convinced that the real baby was either a female or was born dead and that a baby from the immediate neighborhood was substituted in a warming pan. Even the Princess Anne talked in such terms. That James would secure the eventual succession of that child was inevitable unless something were done to stop it. Alternatives were quickly being considered.

For some years the Protestant and anti-French factions in England had considered the ultimate savior to be William of Orange, the husband of Princess Mary, the king's elder daughter and heir (not counting the new baby). William was himself the next heir after Anne, being the son of Mary, the sister of Charles II and James II. William, as stadtholder of the United Netherlands and a Protestant, was the self-proclaimed leader of the opposition to France and Louis XIV in that monarch's attempts to conquer or dominate Western Europe. England had a role to play in his plans. His ideal was that James would retain the throne of a united England; James would allow religious toleration (William himself was relatively tolerant); James would retain his neutrality in foreign policy; and Mary would remain the heir. In time, therefore, William or his wife would inherit the English throne. Many in England hoped to get him involved more openly in favor of the Church of England and in opposition to James's policies. William could not, however, afford to antagonize a strong King James for fear that James would succeed in excluding him from the succession. Although William became increasingly estranged from James as the reign progressed, William would not act until it was safe to do so according to both the English political situation and the continental military situation. By June of 1688 the scene in England was getting out of hand; that on the Continent had immeasurably improved. Louis XIV turned his forces east into the Rhineland and away from the Netherlands. William was now free of the threat from Louis; could he be assured of success in England?

THE INVITATION TO WILLIAM

June 30, 1688, was a remarkable day in England's history. The London court voted to acquit the seven bishops and the "immortal seven" issued their invitation to William. The acquittal was followed by celebrations in the streets of London. The invitation was followed by the orders from William to his forces to prepare for action. Because the willingness to take action in opposition to a lawful king was more in keeping with Whig than with Tory principles, the Glorious Revolution has traditionally been seen as a Whig event and a Whig triumph. It was really an English event and an English triumph, if it can be viewed as being a triumph. The "immortal seven" were in fact three Tories—the earl of Danby, Lord Lumley, and Bishop Compton of London—and four Whigs—the earl of Devonshire, the earl of Shrewsbury, Admiral Edward Russell, and Henry Sidney. The nonpartisan nature of the group was of immense significance. The very people James might have relied upon for support had deserted him. The result was defeat for James and the avoidance of civil war for England. That is why this is referred to as a "Glorious Revolution."

The invitation said that the "religion, liberties and properties" of the people had been threatened by James. In his declaration of September 30, 1688, William said that the "religion, laws, and liberties" of the three kingdoms of England, Scotland, and Ireland had been "overturned" by James. He agreed to take the necessary steps to rectify the situation and called upon all to assist him in this endeavor. No conditions had been required of William before the invitation was issued; he in turn made no specific commitments to any particular group before agreeing to come. William would be in the driver's seat if the landings were successful. They were!

A "Protestant" wind carried William's fleet quickly through the English Channel, and he landed unopposed at Torbay in Devon on November 5, 1688, Guy Fawkes Day. James had already lost the support of his daughter Mary. Anne too quickly deserted her father and rallied to William. So did John Churchill, whom the king had expected to lead the army in his defense. James was almost totally abandoned by his family, his friends, the Church of England, the Tory party, the Dissenters, and the Whigs. He was in a hopeless position and knew it. Although he failed at his first try, he managed to escape to France on the second attempt. Having dropped the Great Seal of England into the Thames, he assumed that no legitimate government could proceed without his return. He totally misread the situation.

WILLIAM TAKES CHARGE

William called a "Convention" parliament into session and it declared, after some sharp debates, that the throne was "vacant." No one would now claim that the baby son of James was king; the debates ignored that possibility. The realistic choices were either to arrange some sort of figurehead role for James or to treat him as if he had died. William and Mary could act as regents for King James. Once that decision was rejected, then the options were that the crown go either to Mary, which was what the Tories wanted, or to William, which is what the Whigs wanted. William himself did not intend to be his "wife's chief usher." He wanted a title sufficiently precise so as to guarantee him the ultimate power to govern. The Tories insisted that by the traditional rules of heredity Mary was queen. To grant the crown to William was to violate the rights of hereditary succession. The exaltation of the powers of Parliament that would justify the alteration of lawful hereditary succession by dint of parliamentary supremacy was fraught with dangers. The Whigs were determined to do just that. William would be eternally grateful to the Whigs, they hoped. Although William was willing to use the Whigs to get the crown, he did not necessarily intend to reign as a parliamentary Whig.

In long and bitter debates the Tories warned the Whigs that too much reliance upon the rights of the nation over the rights of individuals could lead to the extension of the franchise and to parliamentary elections that were far more representative of the population at large than most Whigs really wanted. The final settlement was a compromise. Mary was queen by hereditary right (the Tory claim); William was king by act of Parliament (the Whig claim); William, however, was to rule alone while they reigned jointly.

THE BILL OF RIGHTS

Unlike the Restoration of Charles II in 1660, the Glorious Revolution and the accession of William and Mary to the throne were accompanied by conditions. They were both presented with a Declaration of Rights, which they agreed to in full. This declaration was subsequently presented to Parliament (which the Convention had become) and the Bill of Rights was duly enacted into law. (It has always been called the "Bill of Rights" rather than the "Act of Rights.") The Bill of Rights was largely a restatement of those customary or enacted rights that James had earlier been accused of violating. The most important were the provisions outlawing the right of a king to suspend (repeal) a statute and to dispense with a statute in individual cases.

The most important provision of all was the bestowal of the crown upon William and Mary jointly. This was proof of the ultimate supremacy of Parliament—that it could alter the succession to the throne. Of course any such statute still needed the signature of the reigning monarch. The right to determine who was king or queen did not in and of itself automatically alter the day-to-day role of the monarch in the governance of the realm.

The Bill of Rights also provided for the succession to the throne, everyone being determined to foreclose both the return of James himself and the possible succession of his baby son. The settlement enacted in 1689 called for the survivor of William and Mary to succeed alone. (In 1694 Mary died and William was king on his own.) After their deaths, however, the throne would go to their children. If they together had none, then it would go to any child of Mary. After Mary and her children, it would go to Anne and her children. Then William himself was to have recognition of his own descendants by another wife. That was the end of the list as of 1689. Because William and Mary had no children, and Mary had none by another man and William had none by another woman, the line would descend to Anne.

THE TOLERATION ACT

The Dissenters had been tacitly promised that their refusal to cooperate with James II and acquire toleration by illegal means would be rewarded by the legal granting of toleration once James was out of the picture. The spirit of toleration was demonstrated by the introduction of a Comprehension Bill along with the Toleration Bill. (The former would have restructured the liturgy of the Prayer Book, making one church service for all Englishmen). A similar move had been tried and had failed after the Restoration. It failed again, being turned over to Convocation, which did nothing. The Church of England was to be maintained as it had been in the days of Elizabeth I. If comprehension or the broadening of the liturgy and structure was not to be, then toleration was the answer.

The Toleration Act of 1689 was a far more important event in English history than it has been fashionable for historians to acknowledge. Ever since the Act of Supremacy of 1534, allegiance to the supreme head or governor of the Church of England had been combined with allegiance to the king in his political capacity. The Toleration Act was to end that hitherto necesasry linkage. The relationship between a king and his subjects could now be on a political level only, at least for some of his subjects, if not all of them.

The earlier penal laws against Dissenters were not formally repealed but would not be enforced against those Dissenters who otherwise met the new conditions. To qualify for toleration, the laity among the Dissenters had to swear allegiance to William and Mary and to swear an oath of repugnance to transubstantiation. For Dissenter clergy to qualify, they had to swear allegiance to the Thirty-nine Articles (except those related to the homilies, traditions of the church, and the consecration of bishops). They were also to be excluded from serving in parish offices and on juries. (Actually, in this respect they were being treated as though they were Anglican clergy.) The tithe was still to be paid by Dissenters. None of the provisions of this act were to be applied to Roman Catholics.

Dissenters could now worship openly and in public. In fact, their places of worship had to be registered with the diocesan authorities. The Conventicle Act and the Five-Mile Act of the 1660s Clarendon Code were repealed for all practical purposes. The Test Act was not repealed or modified in any way and remained in force until 1829, barring all non-Anglicans from receiving military or naval commissions, university degrees or fellowships, and from service in the king's government. What alone was tolerated was worship for the Dissenters. In an age of faith this was a great deal and a great deal more than many today would understand.

The Toleration Act was not universally welcomed by either the Anglicans or the Dissenters. Many Anglicans came to regret its passage in later years, and especially the growing practice of "occasional conformity" by which Dissenters would qualify for exemption from the rigors of the Test Act by taking communion once a year. Such easygoing enforcement aroused great opposition in the early eighteenth century, leading to a series of crises in the reign of Queen Anne.

But the Toleration Act also created new problems for the Dissenters. The years of intolerance had also been years of hoping for eventual inclusion in a reformed Church of England. The Toleration Act had to be seen as the end of any hope that the Church of England itself would become inclusive rather than being exclusive. Once this was understood, the Dissenters (especially the Presbyterians) had to create their own separate church organizations. Out of nothing a new structure had to be built. All the while, the leaders of the new Dissenting structure were themselves barred from a full public life by the Test Act.

The oaths of allegiance to William and Mary created another form of dissent. About four hundred hitherto Anglican clergy refused to swear the full oaths of allegiance to William and Mary. They were to be known as the "non-jurors," whose religious allegiance to James II according to the principle of nonresistance was paramount over any secular reasons for swearing loyalty to the parliamentary monarchs William and Mary.

THE ACT OF SETTLEMENT, 1701

The final element of the Glorious Revolution was the Act of Settlement of 1701. Even though William had not yet died and Anne had not yet succeeded, it was clear to the elected Tory Parliament that Anne would bear no more children and that the crown would go to a Catholic unless steps were taken to alter the succession. The twin Tory principles of hereditary succession and loyalty to the Church of England were in direct conflict, even more clearly than they had been after the flight of James II. Once they were so clearly confronted with this conflict, the Tories chose to support the church rather than the hereditary principle. This was not such a contentious issue for the Whigs, who already were convinced that Parliament had the right to alter the succession in an emergency. The Tory decision was made to stick to the hereditary principle as closely as was compatible with Protestantism. The succession was awarded to Sophia, the electress of Hanover, who was the daughter of Elizabeth, the countess Palatine of the Rhine, the daughter of James I. All monarchs since have had to swear upon their succession that they are the next blood heir of Sophia of Hanover. They must also be Protestant, and become Anglican upon succession. The act also provided that the right of succession was to be void if there were a marriage to a Catholic. The Protestant religion was firmly established for all time. Even in the more tolerant society of the late twentieth century, no attempt to modify, much less repeal, this Act of Settlement has been brought forth. The Royal Marriage Act of George III's reign barred the benefits of membership of the royal family to anyone marrying without the monarch's consent. When anyone marries a Catholic they retain the title and style of prince or princess but lose all rights of succession to the throne.

The Act of Settlement had provisions that look more positive to modern eyes. The right of judges to hold office on good behavior (generally life tenure) was included in the act. The act also attempted to make even a foreign king reign as an Englishman. William III had continued to be stadtholder of the Netherlands and had spent much of his time and energy in Holland. The Act of Settlement decreed that no monarch under its provisions could go abroad without the consent of Parliament. If the king were not an Englishman upon his accession, he was expected to become one afterwards.

Part of the Revolutionary Settlement but not directly linked with religion were several other statutes. The Mutiny Act of 1689 authorized the use of martial law to govern the army. However, the act was in effect only for one year. Since William III needed an army for many years in order to have English participation in the War of the League of Augsburg, it meant that Parliament had to meet each year in order to renew the Mutiny Act. Thus the custom of annual parliaments was set. While in session, the Parliament would also of course be asked to vote money to pay for the wars. Parliament has been meeting every year ever since, whether the nation was at war or at peace. The Triennial Act of 1694 was almost redundant at the point of its enactment. It called for elections and a session of Parliament every three years. The failure to renew the act for the regulation of the press in 1696 created by default the right to freedom of the press. The fact that Parliament was meeting every year and that men and money in great numbers and amounts were needed made it increasingly important to both the king and to those in Parliament that the ministers who exercised the executive functions of government be men that the king as well as the Commons had confidence in. Already in the reign of William III the outlines of a royal administration "responsible" to the House of Commons was being developed. The Glorious Revolution marked the end of one era and the beginning of a new one. The government of the United Kingdom today is directly descended from the structure put together in the years after 1688.

CONCLUSION

The Glorious Revolution and the Toleration Act were the end of an era. The Revolution and the creation of a "parliamentary" monarchy with toleration for Protestants marked the end of the struggle between church and state, with the role of the monarch being the central issue. The state, through Parliament, had triumphed over both the church and the king. From now on it was possible to be a loyal subject of the king in his capacity as chief of state without being subject to him as supreme governor of the Church of England. This was still a tricky matter, however. What it meant in the most technical sense was that the Dissenter did not actually deny that the king was governor of the Church of England, but that the Dissenter was not a member of the church.

There was another important difference in the king's place in the new order of things because of the parliamentary origins of the reign of William and Mary and of all those who reigned in accordance with the Act of Settlement of 1701. Never again would a king claim the ancient royal power of healing the sick through the act of touching them. This supposed divine power was thought to be an attribute of divine right (hereditary) monarchy. William was king by act of Parliament, not by divine right. He neither claimed the power to heal nor did others attribute it to him. Queen Anne did inherit the throne by hereditary right and did exercise the healing touch. All subsequent monarchs owed their thrones to the Act of Settlement of 1701. None claimed the healing power, although some Scots did suggest that Queen Victoria had such powers.

In the new era that emerged after the Revolution, religion continued to be a central issue, including debates by use of religious language and arguments. But the central issue had changed: the church was unquestionably just one institution among many that comprised the whole state. The church had to fight to hold its own in a world with ever-increasing rivals to its religious monopoly.

Those in England who remained loyal to the Stuart family became known as Jacobites, from the Hebrew word for James. The Hanoverian Succession inspired many who had accepted William and Mary to turn once again to the Stuarts. A Scottish king was preferable to a German one. But deep down, the Jacobites and the supporters of the Hanoverian Succession were fighting for political supremacy within a state already so politicized that majorities in parliamentary elections counted more than the religious leanings of a monarch.

This was, then, the new England, an England in which the monarch would continue to be a prominent, but not dominant, focus for the government, whose chief participants would increasingly be responsible to a majority in the House of Commons. This was not an England concerned with the old questions of whether the king had the *potestas ordinis* or the *potestas jursidictionis*. This was not an England where the Church of England could assume that its debates over religion had any influence beyond its own parochial boundaries, other than the extent to which politicians could use the various arguments for their own political ends in the new arena shared by Whigs and Tories.

The new era ushered in by the Glorious Revolution was one in which the church recognized that it was under attack by the new forces of secularism and toleration. The debates over these issues and the struggles between Jacobites and Hanoverians, between the non-jurors (those who refused to take the oaths of allegiance to William and Mary) and the juring clergy, and over the place of Latitudinarianism (comprehension) and its links with the world of science were the stuff of politics, but politics fought out in elections, in parliamentary debates, and in Privy Council meetings. The struggle for sovereignty was over. The king, supreme in church and state, had lost; politicians now fought for power within the state, of which the church was a branch, whether it liked it or not.

BIBLIOGRAPHICAL ESSAY

Historical studies of church and state usually put the stress upon one or the other, not both, as this book has tried to do. This essay will tend to divide the suggested readings into two groups: the political and constitutional on the one hand, and the religious and devotional on the other. Each will in turn be separated according to the major chronological periods. As has already been shown in the book, during some periods the state was the more central issue, and during others the church was. What bound church and state together was crucial throughout the centuries that were studied. This essay, and its necessary divisions, reflects the general scholarly approach to the subject, not a desire to keep the two subjects in isolated compartments.

No country in the world has done more to make the sources for the study of its history available to scholars around the world than has England. And no period in that history has been more thoroughly documented than the Tudor/Stuart era. Over the years Oxford University Press commissioned leading English and American scholars to compile massive bibliographies of primary and secondary sources for each century, beginning with the sixteenth. For our period, we have *Bibliography of British History: Tudor Period, 1485–1603*, edited by the great American Tudor scholar Conyers Read (2d ed., 1959), and *Bibliography of British History: Stuart Period, 1603–1714*, edited by Anglo-American scholar Godfrey Davies and updated by the American scholar of the seventeenth-century parliaments, Mary Frear Keeler (2d ed., 1970).

The North American Conference on British Studies and Cambridge University Press have published a series of briefer but more current bibliographies, including *Tudor England, 1485–1603*, by the American scholar Mortimer Levine (1968), and *Restoration England, 1660–1689*, by another American scholar, William L. Sachse (1971).

For general European background reading on the sixteenth and seventeenth centuries, there is the classic *Cambridge Modern History* (5 vols., 1902–1907; reprinted 1934). The *New Cambridge Modern History* began to appear in 1956 with volume II, *The Reformation, 1520–1559*. The second edition, edited by Sir Geoffrey Elton, came out in 1990.

There are several multivolume narrative histories of England that have acquired the stature of "classics." Among them is J. A. Froude, *History of England* (12 vols., New York: Scribner, 1870), which covers the years from the fall of Wolsey in 1529 to the death of Elizabeth I in 1603. Others are Samuel Rawson Gardiner, *History of England from the Accession of James I to the Outbreak of the Civil War, 1603–42* (10 vols., 1883–84), his *History of the Great Civil War, 1642–49,* (3 vols., 1886; rev. 4-vol. ed., 1893), and his *History of the Commonwealth and Protectorate (1649–56)* (3 vols., 1894–1901; 4 vols. from 1903). The last Gardiner work was completed by the equally great researcher and narrator, Sir Charles Harding Firth, in *The Last Years of the Protectorate* (2 vols., 1909). Godfrey Davies considered his *The Restoration of Charles II, 1658–1660* (London, 1955) to be the concluding volume to the Gardiner-Firth enterprise.

The greatest of all the "classic" histories of England is Thomas Babington Macaulay, *The History of England, from the Accession of James II* (5 vols., New York: United States Book Co., 1849–1865). Firth prepared an illustrated edition of Macaulay (6 vols., 1913–15). Not on Macaulay's level, but nonetheless magisterial, are the narratives by David Ogg, *England in the Reign of Charles II* (2 vols., Oxford, 1934), and *England in the Reigns of James II and William III* (Oxford, 1955).

The Oxford History of England series covers the sixteenth and seventeenth centuries in four solid volumes, each of which surveys the political, economic, diplomatic, social, cultural, and religious life of the period, and concludes with very comprehensive bibliographies. The Tudor period is covered by J. D. Mackie in *The Earlier Tudors, 1485–1558* (1952), and J. B. Black, *The Reign of Elizabeth, 1558–1603* (2d ed., 1959). The Stuart century is studied by Godfrey Davies in *The Early Stuarts, 1603–1660* (2d ed., 1959), and Sir George Clark in *The Later Stuarts, 1660–1714* (2d ed., 1956).

Cambridge University Press has provided two documentary histories of the constitution, excerpting important statutes, court cases, parliamentary debates, letters, etc. Each was compiled and introduced by a major scholar of the period. *The Tudor Constitution: Documents and Commentary* was compiled by G. R. Elton (1968), and *The Stuart Constitution: Documents and Commentary* was compiled by J. P. Kenyon (1966).

There is a wide body of scholarly literature covering the pre-Reformation era in England. An excellent place to begin is with the writings of J. N. Figgis, particularly *The Theory of the Divine Right of Kings* (Cambridge, 1896), and *Political Thought from Gerson to Grotius, 1414–1625* (rev. ed. by Garrett Mattingly, New York, 1960). Figgis clearly shows the late medieval links between church and state and how the state came to replace the church as the central locus of authority. A recent detailed analysis of the operations of the church and its relationship with the state is R. N. Swanson, *Church and Society in Late Medieval England* (Oxford, 1989). R. W. Southern, *Western Society and the Church in the Middle Ages* (Baltimore, 1970) is also very helpful.

For background on the Lollards and the influence of John Wycliffe there are several books that put the movement into a wider context: K. B. McFarlane, *John Wycliffe and the Beginning of English Non-Conformity* (London, 1952); J. A. Robson, *Wyclif and the Oxford Schools* (Cambridge, 1961); G. M. Trevelyan, *England in the Age of Wycliffe* (Oxford, 1920); M. Aston, *Lollards and Reformers: Images and Literacy in Late Medieval England* (London, 1984); and a major study of the Lollards and the world of politics, K. B. McFarlan, *Lancastrian Kings and Lollard Knights* (Oxford, 1972). The transition to the Tudor era is studied in J. A. F. Thomson, *The Later Lollards, 1414–1520* (Oxford, 1965).

Two important works study the transition from the late medieval era to the establishment of the early Tudor dynasty: B. P. Wolffe, *Yorkist and Early Tudor Government, 1461–1509* (London, 1966), and J. R. Lander, *Government and Community: England, 1450–1509* (Cambridge, Mass., 1981). There are other books that cover the religious history of this period of transition: C. M. Barron and C. Harper-Bill, eds., *The Church in Pre-Reformation Society* (Rochester, N.Y., 1986); R. B. Dobson, *The Church, Politics, and Patronage in the Fifteenth Century* (Gloucester, Mass., 1984);

L. C. Gabel, *Benefit of Clergy in England in the Late Middle Ages* (Northampton, Mass., 1928); G. Leff, *Heresy in the Late Middle Ages* (2 vols., Manchester, 1967); F. D. Logan, *Excommunication and the Secular Arm in Medieval England: A Study in Legal Procedure from the Thirteenth to the Sixteenth Century* (Toronto, 1968); and W. E. Lunt, *Financial Relations of the Papacy with England, 1327–1534* (Cambridge, Mass., 1962).

The importance of the late medieval Franciscan order is presented in J. R. H. Moorman, *A History of the Franciscan Order from Its Origins to the Year 1517* (Oxford, 1968). Liturgical variations are described in R. W. Pfaff, *New Liturgical Feasts in Late Medieval England* (Oxford, 1970). The great early leader in the field of women's history, Eileen Power, wrote *Medieval English Nunneries, c. 1275 to 1535* (Cambridge, 1922). A very important legal treatise is provided by S. Raban, *Mortmain Legislation and the English Church, 1279–1500* (Cambridge, 1982). A good summation of the period is F. Oakley, *The Western Church in the Late Middle Ages*, Ithaca, N.Y., 1979.

The increasing interest in the intellectual life of the late middle ages was triggered by Johan Huizinga, *The Waning of the Middle Ages* (London, 1924). Three recent studies have followed through by showing the great changes that took place as the medieval world broke down: J. A. H. Moran, *The Growth of English Schooling, 1340–1548: Learning, Literacy, and Laicization in Pre-Reformation York Diocese* (Princeton, 1984); M. A. Mullett, *Popular Culture and Popular Protest in Late Medieval and Early Modern Europe* (London, 1987); and G. R. Owst, *Literature and Pulpit in Medieval England: A Neglected Chapter in the History of English Letters and of the English People* (2d ed., Oxford, 1961). R. C. Finucane studies popular religion in *Miracles and Pilgrims: Popular Belief in Medieval England* (London, 1977).

Administrative issues in the late medieval period are dealt with in R. E. Rodes, Jr., *Ecclesiastical Administration in Medieval England: The Anglo-Saxons to the Reformation* (Notre Dame, Ind., 1977); R. L. Storey, *Diocesan Administration in Fifteenth-Century England* (2d ed., New York, 1972); J. A. F. Thomson, *Popes and Princes, 1417–1517: Politics and Polity in the Late Medieval Church* (London, 1980); W. E. Wilkie, *The Cardinal Protector of England: Rome and the Tudors before the Reformation* (Cambridge, 1974); and R. M. Wunderli, *London Church Courts and Society on the Eve of the Reformation* (Cambridge, Mass., 1981).

For a general survey of the Tudor century, the best one-volume study is still G. R. Elton, *England under the Tudors* (London, 1956), and the most complete description of the actual workings of the Tudor government is Penry Williams, *The Tudor Regime* (Oxford, 1979). The principal source for official work at the royal court is J. S. Brewer, James Gairdner, and R. H. Brodie, eds., *Letters and Papers, Foreign and Domestic, of the Reign of Henry VIII* (21 vols., London, 1862–1910).

Biography is a popular medium for the study of Tudor history. Henry VIII has been a favorite subject, and many books about him were written for nonscholarly audiences. There are a few biographies that have become indispensable for the serious study of Henry's reign and have, in fact, become classics in the genre. The first is A. F. Pollard, *Henry VIII* (London, 1902). A marvelous example of psychohistory is Lacey Baldwin Smith, *Henry VIII: The Mask of Royalty* (London, 1971). The current standard, which charted new ground by thoroughly researching the Vatican archives, is J. J. Scarisbrick, *Henry VIII* (Berkeley and Los Angeles, 1968). Scarisbrick's study of the canon law of divorce and the correspondence between England and the papacy has strengthened the argument that Henry sought to expand his power within England, even if that meant a challenge to papal authority within England. Scarisbrick decidedly takes the position that the Reformation in England was from "the top down." It was imposed; it did not spring up from the ground. The opposite view, that the seeds of the Reformation had already been planted in fertile soil, can be found in A. G. Dickens, *The English Reformation* (London, 1964) and in his more recent detailed study of the impact of the Lollard movement upon early Tudor England, *Lollards and Protestants in the Diocese of York, 1509–1555* (London, 1982).

That Scarisbrick is a Catholic and Dickens a Protestant may not be irrelevant to the debate. Since the sixteenth century, Protestant historians have stressed that being Protestant was in the natural order of things. If it had not happened when and how it did, it would have happened eventually, one way or another. Catholic historians have not accepted this inevitability of a Protestant England; quite the contrary. Until the twentieth century, in fact, little serious Catholic historical scholarship was being produced on this issue. Henry was passed off in popular tracts as an adulterous, tyrannical, murderous heretic. The first serious Catholic scholar to tackle the English Reformation was Fr. Philip Hughes in *The Reformation in England* (3 vols., London, 1950–1954). This has been recognized as a thoroughly balanced account. Scarisbrick soon replaced him as the leading scholar of Henry VIII and has followed up on his biography of Henry and the depth of Henry's influence in his most recent book, *The Reformation and the English People* (Oxford, 1984). In this short book Scarisbrick clearly shows that England was Catholic throughout the reign of Henry VIII and that the comprehensive nature of the Elizabethan Settlement was because the people were still Catholic even though Protestantism was imposed from above. Scarisbrick's conclusion is that if England were destined to be Protestant, it could only be in the Anglican (via media) mold. England, then, was destined to be Anglican only if it could not remain Catholic. Christopher Haigh also stressed this continuity with Catholicism in *The English Reformation Revised* (Cambridge, 1987).

The English Reformation has been studied both as a whole or in any of its topical and chronological parts. The usual way to divide it is to treat the period of the break from Rome and the establishment of the royal supremacy as one part, the Elizabethan Settlement as a second part, and the rise of Puritanism, which led to civil war and revolution, as a third part. The post-Restoration era and the Glorious Revolution are often treated as separate periods, and not always related to what preceded them. This book has attempted to rectify that by showing that what began in 1529 did not end until 1689. The traditional chronological divisions will be recognized for the purposes of this bibliographical essay, beginning, however, with reference to those books that have taken a longer view. The most recent is Leo Solt, *Church and State in Early Modern England, 1509–1640* (Oxford, 1990). Another such sweeping survey, which includes relations with the European continent, is Derek Baker, *Reform and Reformation: England and the Continent, c. 1500–1750* (Oxford, 1979). Felicity Heal and Rosemary O'Day have written two very useful books: *Church and Society in*

England, Henry VIII to James I (London, 1977), and *Continuity and Change: Personnel and Administration of the Church of England, 1500–1642* (Leicester, 1976).

A sweeping history of the Bible is found in *The Cambridge History of the Bible*, vol. III, *The World from the Reformation to the Present Day* (Cambridge, 1963). An equally sweeping history of the liturgy is in Paul F. Bradshaw, *The Anglican Ordinal, Its History and Development from the Reformation to the Present Day* (London, 1971).

The best complete one-volume survey of the reign of Henry VIII is H. Maynard Smith, *Henry VIII and the Reformation* (London, 1964). Smith, a clergyman, is not concerned primarily with the issues that bothered historians, focusing instead on practical religious matters. The initiation of the divorce and its consequences are thoroughly covered in G. de C. Parmiter, *The King's Great Matter: A Study of Anglo-Papal Relations, 1527–1534* (London, 1967). A. F. Pollard, *Wolsey* (London, 1929) is still worth reading, although it is out of date on the role of the papacy. The role played by Thomas Cromwell after the fall of Wolsey is thoroughly documented in several books by Sir Geoffrey Elton, especially *Reform and Reformation, England, 1509–1585* (Cambridge, Mass., 1977), and *Reform and Renewal, Thomas Cromwell and the Commonweal*, (Cambridge, Mass., 1973). The roles played by Henry and Cromwell in Parliament are thoroughly explored in two fine books by Stanford E. Lehmberg, *The Reformation Parliament* (Cambridge, 1970), and *The Later Parliaments of Henry VIII, 1536–1547* (Cambridge, 1977). The enforcement of the Reformation and the opposition to it are studied in G. R. Elton, *Policy and Police, the Enforcement of the Reformation in the Age of Thomas Cromwell* (Cambridge, 1972).

There are two excellent biographies of Archbishop Thomas Cranmer. One is the old classic by A. F. Pollard, *Thomas Cranmer and the English Reformation* (London, 1904). The other, more recent, is by Jasper Ridley, *Thomas Cranmer* (Oxford, 1962). There is also an old but still useful biography, *Stephen Gardiner and the Tudor Reaction* by J. A. Muller (London, 1926). E. W. Ives has provided a scholarly biography of *Anne Boleyn* (Oxford, 1986), and Lacey Baldwin Smith has surveyed the clergy up to the accession of Elizabeth in *Tudor Prelates and Politics, 1536–1558*

(Princeton, N. J., 1953). The principal biography of Sir Thomas More is still R. W. Chambers, *Thomas More* (London, 1935), and that of Hugh Latimer is H. Chester, *Hugh Latimer, Apostle to the English* (Philadelphia, 1954). A Catholic view of Cranmer is Hilaire Belloc, *Cranmer* (London, 1931).

The political theories associated with the Reformation are thoroughly surveyed in the classic by J. W. Allen, *History of Political Thought in the Sixteenth Century* (London, rev. ed., 1957), and in Franklin Le Van Baumer, *The Early Tudor Theory of Kingship* (New Haven, Conn., 1940) and W. G. Zeeveld, *Foundations of Tudor Policy* (Cambridge, Mass., 1948). Political theory is related to the royal supremacy in E. T. Davies, *Episcopacy and the Royal Supremacy in the Church of England in the XVIth Century* (Oxford, 1950).

The dissolution of the monasteries and chantries has been treated in several books. The first major Protestant study is Geoffrey Baskerville, *English Monks and the Suppression of the Monasteries* (London, 1937). A classic Roman Catholic view is F. A. Gasquet, *Henry VIII and the English Monasteries* (2 vols., London, 1906). A more recent study of the chantries is Alan Kreider, *English Chantries: The Road to Destruction* (Cambridge, Mass., 1979). The best book covering the whole issue is Joyce Youing, *The Dissolution of the Monasteries* (London, 1971).

The reign of the boy king Edward VI has been thoroughly covered in the two-volume biography by W. K. Jordan, *Edward VI: The Young King* (London, 1968), and *Edward VI: The Threshold of Power* (London, 1970). The biographies of Cranmer are especially useful for study of this reign, as are histories of the Prayer Books, such as F. A. Gasquet and E. Bishop, *Edward VI and the Book of Common Prayer* (London, 1890). The history and theology of the Prayer Books are also dealt with in detail in works that go beyond the years of Cranmer, such as G. J. Cumings, *A History of Anglican Liturgy* (London, 1969), and Horton Davies, *Worship and Theology in England from Cranmer to Hooker, 1534–1603,* (Oxford, 1970). Cranmer's borrowings from the Salisbury liturgy are detailed in W. H. Frere, *The Use of Sarum* (2 vols., Cambridge, 1895–1901). Cranmer's theology is analyzed afresh in Peter Brooks, *Thomas Cranmer's Doctrine of the Eucharist, an Essay in Historical Development* (New York, 1965).

The reign of Mary Tudor and the Catholic restoration have aroused controversy over the question of what role the queen herself played in the executions for heresy. Most historians find her to be not totally blameless and, at the same time, an object of pity. The most balanced biography is H. F. M. Prescott, *Mary Tudor* (New York, 1953). A leading scholar of the reign is D. M. Loades, who wrote *The Reign of Mary Tudor* (New York, 1979), and *The Oxford Martyrs* (New York, 1970). The best biography of Mary's archbishop of Canterbury is W. Schenk, *Reginald Pole* (London, 1950). The matter of heresy in one region is dealt with in J. F. Davis, *Heresy and Reformation in the South East of England, 1520–1559* (London, 1983).

The broader intellectual background to the Reformation and its links with Renaissance humanism are explored in two books: M. Dowling, *Humanism in the Age of Henry VIII* (London, 1986) and J. K. McConica, *English Humanists and Reformation under Henry VIII and Edward VI* (Oxford, 1965). Elizabeth L. Eisenstein has made a major contribution in her two-volume study, *The Printing Press as an Agent of Change: Communications and Cultural Transformations in Early Modern Europe* (Cambridge, 1979). This is a pioneer work on the influence of technology on the religious and intellectual life of early modern Europe.

The reign of Elizabeth I has generated a vast amount of historical writing, much of which stresses either the relationship between the Anglican establishment and the Puritans or the relationship between the church in general and the wider society, both of which include, of course, the role of the royal court and its relationship with Parliament. The reigns of Henry VIII and Edward VI did not see the creation of the modern Church of England; this was the work of Elizabeth I and her ministers, lay and clerical, in the first years of the reign. Elizabeth herself never articulated a clear religious position, but no scholar can deny that one way or another she had a determining influence on what was or was not done. The classic biography is J. E. Neale, *Queen Elizabeth I* (London, 1934). Her relationships with Parliament are detailed in J. E. Neale's two volumes, *Elizabeth I and Her Parliaments* (London, 1953–1957). Neale, an English scholar, had discovered a great deal of hitherto unknown manuscript material. His American counterpart, Conyers Read, has also discovered manuscript sources for the study of the queen's chief ministers. Read has written five detailed and important books: *Mr. Secretary Cecil and Queen Elizabeth* (New York, 1955); *Lord Burghley and Queen Elizabeth* (New York, 1960); *Mr. Secretary Walsingham and the Policy of Queen Elizabeth* (3 vols., Oxford, 1925). More recently G. R. Elton has produced the first volume in his revision of Neale, *The Parliament of England, 1559–1581* (Cambridge, 1986).

The most detailed analysis of theology for this period is the previously cited work by Horton Davies, *Worship and Theology in England from Cranmer to Hooker, 1534–1603* (Princeton, N.J., 1970). The most detailed study of the Thirty-nine Articles is E. J. A. Bicknell, *A Theological Introduction to the Thirty-Nine Articles of the Church of England* (2d ed., London, 1942). The struggle within the establishment itself over Puritan demands for reform is covered in Patrick Collinson, *Archbishop Grindal, 1519–1583, the Struggle for a Reformed Church* (Berkeley, 1980). The challenges to the Elizabethan establishment have generated much more historical writing than has the defense of that establishment.

The rise of Puritanism in Elizabethan England traditionally has been viewed as the preparation for the grander struggle between the parliamentary and royal authorities that climaxed in the Puritan Revolution of 1640–1660. Christian H. Garrett has shown the link between Puritanism and those exiled in Mary Tudor's reign in *The Marian Exiles, A Study in the Origins of Elizabethan Puritanism* (Cambridge, 1966). One of the first books to look at some of the less famous Puritan figures is Marshall Knappen, *Tudor Puritanism* (Chicago, 1939). A more comprehensive survey, which has achieved the stature of a classic, is William Haller, *The Rise of Puritanism* (New York, 1938). A broad view of Elizabethan Puritanism is provided in Peter Lake, *Moderate Puritans and the Elizabethan Church* (Cambridge, 1982). The relationship between the Puritans and the Catholics was provided in Patrick McGrath, *Papists and Puritans under Elizabeth I* (London, 1967). The last years of the Elizabethan movement are summed up in Peter Lake, *Anglicans and Puritans? Presbyterianism and English Conformist Thought from Whitgift to Hooker* (London, 1988). The relationship of the Puritans with separatism is studied in Stephen Brachlow, *The Communion of Saints, Radical Puritan and Separatist Ecclesiology, 1570–1625* (Oxford, 1988).

Excellent biographies of Elizabeth's first and last archbishops of Canterbury, both by V. J. K. Brook, are *A Life of Archbishop Parker* (Oxford, 1962), and *Whitgift and the English Church* (London, 1957). Whitgift's role also is studied in P. M. Dawley's *John Whitgift and the English Reformation* (New York, 1954).

The political challenge to the crown from Puritanism is portrayed in Leland H. Carlson, ed., *Martin Marprelate, Gentleman, Master Job Throckmorton Laid Open in His Colors*, (San Marino, Calif., 1981), and in Claire Cross, *The Royal Supremacy in the Elizabethan Church* (London, 1969). A more generalized intellectual view of the church-state conflict can be found in Stephen L. Collins, *From Divine Cosmos to Sovereign State: An Intellectual History of Consciousness and the Idea of Order in Renaissance England* (Oxford, 1991).

The Puritan links with image smashing have been covered in a pioneer work by John Phillips, *The Reformation of Images: Destruction of Art in England, 1535–1660* (Berkeley, 1973), and more recently in a fine book by Stanford E. Lehmberg, *The Reformation of Cathedrals: Cathedrals in English Society, 1485–1603* (Cambridge, 1989). Margaret Aston's major multivolume study has also begun to appear: *England's Iconoclasts*, volume I: *Laws against Images* (Oxford, 1988).

The place of Roman Catholics in the newly Protestant England has received much attention. Multicentury surveys are found in John Bossy, *The English Catholic Community, 1570–1850* (New York, 1976), and Thomas H. Clancy, *Papist Pamphleteers, the Allen-Persons Party and the Political Thought of the Counter-Reformation in England, 1572–1615* (Chicago, 1964). Catholic and Protestant differences are reviewed in C. W. Dugmore, *The Mass and the English Reformers* (London, 1958). Garrett Mattingly, *The Armada* (Boston, 1959) is a marvelous story of the complex relationships, political and religious, within England and throughout Western Europe. The best work on the place of Catholicism in the seventeenth century is Martin Havran, *The Catholics in Caroline England* (Stanford, Calif., 1962).

There are several books that provide a transition from the Elizabethan age to the early Stuart periods. A detailed study of theology is another book by Horton Davies, *Worship and Theology in England, from Andrews to Baxter and Fox, 1603–1690* (Princeton, N.J., 1975). A detailed study of the administration of the church in the north of England is found in R. M. Marchant, *The Church under the Law: Justice, Administration and Discipline in the Diocese of York, 1560–1640* (Cambridge, 1969). There are two excellent surveys by Patrick Collinson of the social impact of religion: *The Religion of Protestants: The Church in English Society, 1559–1626* (Oxford, 1982), and *Godly People: Essays on English Protestantism and Puritanism* (London, 1983). Another survey, which stresses the "via media" theme, is C. H. and K. George, *The Protestant Mind of the English Reformation, 1570–1640* (Princeton, N.J., 1961). A major study of the struggle between a largely Puritan church and the Arminian opposition to it is Nicholas Tyacke, *Anti-Calvinists: The Rise of English Arminianism, c. 1590–1640* (Oxford, 1987). A brilliant study of the Puritan mind and the triumph of Oliver Cromwell is Michael Walzer, *The Revolution of the Saints* (Cambridge, Mass., 1965). A rebuttal to Collinson's view that the Church of England was really Puritan is found in Dewey D. Wallace, Jr., *Puritans and Predestination, Grace in English Protestant Theology* (Chapel Hill, N. C., 1982).

The role of Archbishop Bancroft in the reign of James I is covered by S. B. Babbage in *Puritanism and Richard Bancroft* (London, 1962). An excellent collection of essays on the importance of Richard Hooker is W. Speed Hill, ed., *Studies in Richard Hooker, Essays Preliminary to an Edition of His Works* (Cleveland, 1972). The political implications of Puritanism during the period are discussed by Paul S. Seaver in *The Puritan Lectureship: The Politics of Religious Dissent, 1560–1662* (Stanford, Calif., 1970). The emerging crisis in church and state is explored in John E. Booty, *John Jewel as Apologist of the Church of England* (London, 1963); E. C. E. Bourne, *The Anglicanism of William Laud* (London, 1947); John F. New, *Anglican and Puritan, the Basis of Their Opposition, 1558–1640* (Stanford, Calif., 1964); and William M. Lamont, *Godly Rule, Politics and Religion, 1603–1660* (London, 1969).

Christopher Hill has provided two important studies of the economic and social circumstances facing the church prior to the

Puritan Revolution: *The Economic Problems of the Church from Whitgift to the Long Parliament* (Oxford, 1956), and *Society and Puritanism in Pre-Revolutionary England* (New York, 1964). Archbishop Laud's efforts to solve the problems confronting the church were brilliantly covered in H. R. Trevor-Roper, *Archbishop Laud* (2d ed., London, 1962). A more recent study is Charles Carlton, *Archbishop William Laud* (London, 1987). The years of Charles I's personal rule are covered in Esther Cope, *Politics without Parliament, 1629–1640* (London, 1987).

The psychology of the Puritan experience has attracted much attention. Michael Walzer, *Revolution of the Saints* (Cambridge, Mass., 1965) has already been cited. C. L. Cohen, *God's Caress, the Psychology of Puritan Religious Experience* (New York, 1966) is very useful. A major survey of the problem is Paul Christianson, *Reformers and Babylon, English Apocalyptic Visions from the Reformation to the Eve of the Civil War* (Toronto, 1978). A somewhat different but not unrelated approach is Charles F. Allison, *The Rise of Moralism: The Proclamation of the Gospel from Hooker to Baxter* (London, 1966). Another version is in Norman Pettit, *The Heart Prepared: Grace and Conversion in Puritan Spiritual Life* (New Haven, Conn., 1966).

The political and religious conflicts that became violent in the civil wars have generated a vast outpouring of books dealing with any and all aspects of the crisis. There are several books devoted to trying to figure out what caused the Puritan or English Revolution and/or the civil wars. The most sweeping is Lawrence Stone, *The Causes of the English Revolution, 1529–1642* (Oxford, 1972). The most controversial is Conrad Russell, *The Causes of the English Civil War* (Oxford, 1990). A useful survey of the history of the various interpretations is R. C. Richardson, *The Debate on the English Revolution Revisited* (New York, 1989). A tour de force linking the historiographical debates over the Puritan Revolution with those over the nature of the eighteenth century and the Reform Bill of 1832 is J. C. D. Clark, *Revolution and Rebellion: State and Society in England in the Seventeenth and Eighteenth Centuries* (Cambridge, 1986).

The best one-volume coverage of the Revolution is Ivan Roots, *The Great Rebellion* (London, 1966). A comprehensive collection of the contemporary documents is found in S. E. Prall, *The Puri-*

tan Revolution: A Documentary History (New York, 1968). The classic biography of Cromwell is still C. H. Firth, *Oliver Cromwell and the Rule of the Puritans in England* (New York, 1900). C. V. Wedgewood has covered the first ten years in three beautifully constructed volumes: *The King's Peace, 1637–41* (New York, 1956); *The King's War* (New York, 1958); and *The Trial of Charles I* (London, 1964).

There is extensive literature on the Commonwealth and the Protectorate, the years of Puritan triumph. An excellent survey of the historiography is Michael G. Finlayson, *Historians, Puritanism and the English Revolution: The Religious Factor in English Politics before and after the Interregnum* (Toronto, 1983). The classic survey of the Puritan attempts to create a new England is William Haller, *Liberty and Reformation in the Puritan Revolution* (New York, 1963). An excellent survey of the religious life of England before, during, and after the Revolution is J. Sears McGee, *The Godly Man in Stuart England: Anglicans, Puritans, and the Two Tables, 1620–1670* (New Haven, Conn., 1976). The military side of Puritanism in action has been well covered in Leo Solt, *Saints in Arms* (Stanford, 1959), and Mark Kishlansky, *The Rise of the New Model Army* (Cambridge, 1979). One man's struggle on both sides of the Atlantic has been portrayed in Raymond Phineas Stearns, *The Strenuous Puritan: Hugh Peters, 1598–1660* (Urbana, Ill., 1954). Puritan political preaching has been carefully covered in John F. Wilson, *Pulpit in Parliament: Puritanism during the English Civil Wars, 1640–1648* (Princeton, N.J., 1969). Two looks at the more extreme end of the religious reformers are Bernard S. Capp, *The Fifth Monarchy Men: A Study in Seventeenth-Century English Millenarianism* (Totowa, N.J., 1972), and David Katz, *Sabbath and Sectarianism in Seventeenth-Century England* (Oxford, 1988).

Two magisterial works sum up the religious experience of the seventeenth century in different but equally challenging ways: W. K. Jordan, *The Development of Religious Toleration in England from the Accession of James I to the Convention of the Long Parliament (1603–1640)* (Cambridge, Mass., 1936); and Sir Keith Thomas, *Religion and the Decline of Magic* (New York, 1971).

The Restoration and the years up to the Glorious Revolution are beginning to receive more attention. The transition from the Puritan Revolution to the Restoration was covered in Robert S. Bosher, *The Making of the Restoration Settlement: The Influence of the Laudians, 1649–1662* (London, 1957). The history of Restoration religious dissent is thoroughly covered in Douglas R. Lacey, *Dissent and Parliamentary Politics in England, 1661–1689: A Study in the Perpetuation and Tempering of Parliamentarianism* (New Brunswick, N.J., 1969). An excellent survey of changing religious ideas for the remainder of the century is found in Gerald R. Cragg, *From Puritanism to the Age of Reason: A Study of Change in Religious Thought within the Church of England, 1660–1770* (Cambridge, 1966). A very helpful collection of essays by several major scholars is Ole Peter Grell, Jonathan I. Israel, and Nicholas Tyacke, *From Persecution to Toleration: The Glorious Revolution in England* (Oxford, 1991). A comprehensive survey is John Spurr, *The Restoration Church of England, 1646–1689* (New Haven, Conn., 1991). The classic history of the royal healing touch is by the great French scholar Marc Bloch, *The Royal Touch: Sacred Monarchy and Scrofula in England and France* (London, 1983).

There are several histories of the Glorious Revolution, beginning with the classic by G. M. Trevelyan, *The English Revolution, 1688–1689* (London, 1938). A more sympathetic view of James II is found in Maurice Ashley, *The Glorious Revolution of 1688* (New York, 1966). Two controversial interpretations claiming that England had been "conquered" by William and the Dutch are Lucile Pinkham, *William III and the Respectable Revolution* (Cambridge, Mass., 1954), and John Carswell, *The Descent on England* (New York, 1969). A fine account of James II's attempts to get a parliament with which he could work for religious toleration is J. R. Jones, *The Revolution of 1688 in England* (New York, 1972). S. E. Prall, *The Bloodless Revolution: England, 1688* (Madison, Wisc., 1985) shows the continuity of issues between the Puritan Revolution and the Glorious Revolution and the extent to which the latter was a joint Whig and Tory endeavor. The long-range view is taken in J. R. Western, *Monarchy and Revolution: The English State in the 1680's* (Totowa, N. J., 1972).

The post-Revolution era is well covered in Gerald Straka, *Anglican Reaction to the Revolution of 1688* (Madison, Wisc., 1962), and in Geoffrey Holmes, *Britain after the Glorious Revolution, 1689–1714* (New York, 1969). The classic analysis of the Bill of Rights is Lois Schwoerer, *The Declaration of Rights* (Baltimore, 1981).

INDEX

173

DATE DUE

FEB 15 '96			
FEB 18 '98			
NOV 2 2 2000			
Chu			
Cop			
Spo			
Pro			Printed in USA
Ind			
Typ			

Printer, McNaughton & Gunn, Inc.
Book designer, Roger Eggers

Stuart E. Prall is a Professor of History at Queens College and the Graduate School and University Center, City University of New York. He is the author of many books and articles, including *A History of England*, which he coauthored with D. H. Willson.